HAWAI'I'S BEST

SALADS, SIDES & SOUPS

Other Books by Jean Watanabe Hee

Hawaiʻi's Best Mochi Recipes

Hawaiʻi's Best Local Desserts

Hawaiʻi's Best Local Dishes

Hawaiʻi's Best Pūpū & Potluck

Tastes & Flavors of Mochi

HAWAI'I'S BEST

SALADS, SIDES & SOUPS

Jean Watanabe Hee

MUTUAL PUBLISHING

ISBN-10: 1-56647-781-6
ISBN-13: 978-1-56647-781-9

First Printing, September 2006
Second Printing, November 2007

Mutual Publishing, LLC
1215 Center Street, Suite 210
Honolulu, Hawai'i 96816
Ph: 808-732-1709 / Fax: 808-734-4094
email: info@mutualpublishing.com
www.mutualpublishing.com

Printed in Korea

Dedication

To my wonderful granddaughters,
Rachel and Kristen Hasegawa.
This cookbook is dedicated to you.
I hope you will enjoy more soups
and salads with your meals.

Table of Contents

Acknowledgments

I want to thank all my relatives, friends and neighbors who have been positive and supportive in all my projects. I especially want to thank Evelyn Shiraki, my neighbor across the street, who really went out of her way to bring to my attention certain recipes that she felt were excellent. One example was the "Country Comfort Corn Chowder" which she tasted while visiting her son, Jerry, and his family in Kamuela on the Big Island. She prepared the soup, brought it over and let me taste it. When I raved about it she gave me the recipe and also told me how to contact Lisa Fujioka whose original recipe it was.

Another example was a daikon koko recipe that her mother, Dot Inoue, had passed on to her. It is a good recipe. But when her cousin came to visit one day with a jar of her homemade takuan, Evelyn thought it was even better. Again, she brought over a sample to see what I thought. So that new recipe, "Takuan," is now in this cookbook.

I also want to thank Audry Mijo, my next door neighbor, for her support and help whenever I needed it. She gave me good feedback on some of the recipes. Her daughter, Coreen, also recommended a soup popular with young adults. She cooked it and let me taste it. The "Black Bean Soup" is quick and easy to prepare and is spicy and full of flavor.

Over on the Big Island, Roger Pflum was so generous and helpful in sharing his recipes and cookbooks with me. He is an avid cook and is willing to try anything. I learned a lot from him. I am so thankful that he shared his favorite: steamed chicken and tomato soup, "Ga Hap Ca," with me. It is so delicious. You must try it.

And on Maui, Glen Oura shared some recipes, one of which was a creation of poke, Chinese cabbage, walnuts and raisins. At a supermarket, Eleanor Tokunaga shared her "Hearty Miso Soup." I want to thank you and all the others too numerous to mention who helped by contributing recipes for this cookbook. I enjoyed testing and tasting them.

Introduction

This cookbook was a direct request three years ago from my daughter, Cheryl. At that time her two young daughters' favorite meal for breakfast and lunch included some kind of soup. They enjoyed a little cooked rice in a bowl with soup poured over. They preferred that to pancakes or cereal or sandwiches.

Another good reason for preparing soup is that you could throw in all kinds of vegetables and, softened, you could blend them into the rice and that way the children would eat them. The younger daughter, you see, did not like to eat anything with green color. So, soup is nutritious, warm and soft and easy to swallow.

It took a while because of certain personal events that happened during the last two years but even though my granddaughters are older I know they are going to enjoy the many different soups that their mother will prepare for the family using the recipes gathered together in this cookbook.

I thoroughly enjoyed testing and tasting the many recipes. A pleasant discovery was the many ways miso soup was being enjoyed. I was used to basic miso soup with broth, miso, tofu and green onions. I found there were so many variations. Included in this cookbook are some of the miso soups that include more vegetables and even spare ribs.

My friends, who are my age, requested more salad and vegetable dishes. We are more aware of eating healthy and, also, we are finding that as we grow older we prefer eating less meat and more vegetable dishes. So I also included a salad section and a sides section.

I hope you enjoy these recipes. All recipes are tested and I tried to write them so they would be easy to follow.

Soups

Asian Flavored Chicken Soup

yield: 8–10 servings

* *

4 to 5 pounds chicken
3 quarts water
1 tablespoon salt
1 large onion (will be strained out)
4 ribs celery with leaves (will be strained out)
4 carrots (will be strained out)

Trim fat and cut chicken into large pieces. Place in large soup pot; cover with water. Add salt. Heat to boiling; skim froth from surface. Add onion and celery; simmer on low heat for 1 hour. Add carrots; simmer for another hour. Remove large vegetable pieces and strain stock. Separate chicken meat and discard bones and cartilage. Let cool. Refrigerate chicken and broth in separate containters overnight. Skim solidified fat in the morning.

1/4 teaspoon sesame oil
1 tablespoon fresh ginger, minced
1 tablespoon garlic, minced
1 teaspoon oyster sauce
2 to 3 carrots, sliced
1 potato, sliced
1 bunch dark leafy greens (e.g., kale, bok choy, etc.),
    roughly cut

Sauté chicken meat quickly with sesame oil, ginger, garlic and oyster sauce. Add to soup. Add carrot and potato slices; simmer until potatoes are cooked. Add greens just before serving to wilt, but do not overcook.

Optional: Garnish with Chinese parsley or fresh basil.

Mushroom Soup

yield: 6 servings

* *

4 cans chicken broth (14.5 oz. each)
3 tablespoons soy sauce
3 cloves garlic, crushed
2 teaspoons grated fresh ginger
4 cups assorted mushrooms, sliced (e.g., white buttons, portobello, crimini, shiitake)
1 large carrot, sliced
1/4 head cabbage, cut in wedges
1 pound boneless, skinless chicken breast or thighs, thinly sliced
2 cups fresh udon noodles (or substitute 2 cups cooked linguine)
1 to 2 stalks green onions, thinly sliced
2 cups spinach leaves, shredded
Black pepper to taste
1 tablespoon mirin (optional)

In large pot, combine chicken broth, soy sauce, garlic, ginger, mushrooms, carrot and cabbage. Cover; bring to boil. Add chicken and simmer until mushrooms are soft, about 5 minutes. Stir in noodles, green onions and spinach. Simmer 2 minutes more or until greens are wilted. Season with pepper and mirin to taste.

Note: Eloise Yano recommended this healthy soup of mushrooms which may help to boost immunity, fend off infections and may have anti-cancer properties and other benefits. This soup is also tasty. Eloise says this is a good dish to give to those who are ill. She uses a package of ready to use Udon Noodles (7.22-oz.) (e.g. Myojo® brand found on most grocery shelves; do not use the soup seasoning packet, however).

Hint: If using dried shiitake, soak in warm water until softened and discard stems. Portobello tends to make the soup a darker color so you may not want to include it.

Black Bean Soup

yield: 12–15 servings

* *

2 cans whole kernel corn (15 oz. each), drained
2 cans black beans (15 oz. each), drain only one can
2 cans diced tomatoes with green chilies (14.5 oz. each)
2 cans chicken broth (14.5 oz. each)
2 cans chunk chicken in water (10 oz. each), or
    meat from 1 roast chicken, chopped (about 3 cups)
Black pepper to season

Combine all ingredients and bring to boil; simmer 5 minutes.

Note: This soup, a little on the spicy side, is quite popular with young adults. It is very tasty and so quick and easy to prepare. My young neighbor, Coreen Mijo, got this recipe from her friend, Debbie Murata, and shared it with me.

Chicken Broth

yield: 4–6 servings

* *

3 to 3-1/2 pounds cut-up broiler-fryer chicken
5 cups water
1 stalk celery with leaves, cut up
1 carrot, cut up
1 small onion, cut up
1 sprig parsley
1 teaspoon salt
1/2 teaspoon pepper

Remove excess fat from chicken. Place chicken in large pot (except liver). Add remaining ingredients. Heat to boiling; skim foam from broth. Reduce heat to low. Cover and simmer until chicken is cooked (about 45 minutes).

Remove chicken from broth. Cool chicken about 10 minutes or just until cool enough to handle. Remove skin and bones from chicken. Cut chicken into 1/2-inch pieces.

Strain broth through cheesecloth lined sieve; discard vegetables. Skim fat from broth. Use immediately or refrigerate broth and chicken in separate containers up to 24 hours. May be frozen for future use.

Chicken Noodle Soup

yield: 4 – 6 servings

✳ ✳

5 cups chicken broth (see recipe on page 5 for chicken broth).
2 medium carrots, sliced
1 to 2 stalks celery, sliced
1 small onion, chopped
1 tablespoon chicken bouillon granules
1 cup uncooked medium noodles
1 cup cooked chicken, cut into 1/2-inch pieces
Salt and pepper to taste

Add enough water to fresh chicken broth, if necessary, to measure 5 cups. Heat broth, carrots, celery, onion and bouillon granules to boiling; reduce heat to low. Cover and simmer until carrots are tender (about 15 minutes). Stir in noodles and chicken. Heat to boiling. Reduce heat to low; simmer, uncovered, until noodles are tender (about 7 to 10 minutes). Season with salt and pepper to your taste.

Variation: Substitute noodles with 1/2 cup uncooked rice for chicken rice soup. Stir in rice with the vegetables. Cover and simmer until rice is tender (about 15 minutes). Add chicken and heat until chicken is hot.

Chicken–Tomato Soup

yield: 12–14 servings

* *

2 cans chicken broth (15 oz. each)
2 cans stewed tomatoes (14.5 oz. each), chopped
1 can pinto beans (15 oz.)
1 cup salsa, any brand (adjust to taste)
1 can whole kernel corn (7 oz.)
1 can sliced black olives (2.25 oz.), drained
2 tablespoons basil
1 teaspoon cumin

Combine ingredients in pot. Bring to boil and simmer for approximately 1 hour.

Easy Egg Flower Drop Soup

yield: 6 servings

* *

2 cans chicken broth (14.5 oz. each)
1 can cream style corn (14.75 oz.)
1 egg, beaten

Heat chicken broth; stir in corn. Bring to boil; stir in beaten egg.

Note: Glenn Oura, who lives on Maui, shared this easy recipe with me.

Chicken Papaya Soup

yield: 6 servings

* *

1 pound boneless and skinless chicken thighs,
    cut into 1-inch pieces
1/2 pound shrimp with shells on (31 to 40 count),
    deveined and washed
2 tablespoons butter
2 cloves garlic, crushed
6 cups water
1/2 teaspoon salt (adjust to taste)
1-1/2 pounds green papayas, peeled,
    seeded and cut into 1-inch cubes

Heat butter in large saucepan; sauté garlic and ginger with chicken and shrimp. Add water and salt. Cover and simmer until chicken is tender (about 45 minutes). Add papaya and cook until papaya is tender (about 15 minutes).

Note: Sautéed shrimp may be removed and set aside before adding water. Return shrimp to pot when adding papaya.

Hint: Papaya must be totally green and flesh must be white. There should not be any yellow or orange tint to papaya.

Chinese Cabbage Soup

yield: 4 – 6 servings

* *

3 to 4 ounces lean pork, finely sliced

Marinade:

1 teaspoon cornstarch
2 teaspoons soy sauce
1/2 teaspoon sugar
1/4 teaspoon pepper

Combine marinade ingredients and marinate pork at least 15 minutes.

Vegetable oil
2 to 3 thin slices ginger
1 teaspoon salt
6 cups boiling water
4 cups Chinese cabbage, coarsely sliced

Heat a little oil in pot, just enough to grease bottom of pot. Fry ginger and salt for 30 seconds. Pour in 6 cups of boiling water. Cover pot with lid and simmer for 8 minutes. Add seasoned pork; simmer for 10 minutes, skimming off "scum." Remove ginger slices. Add Chinese cabbage; simmer another 5 minutes or until cabbage is cooked to your taste.

Note: Basic simple Chinese soup is generally made with lean pork marinated at least 15 minutes. When using soup bones of any type of meat, cover with water and cook at least 1-1/2 hours before adding seasoning and vegetables.

Chinese Chicken Soup

yield: 10 servings

* *

1 chicken breast or 2 chicken thighs, skinless
    and boneless, sliced
2 teaspoons cornstarch
1 teaspoon sesame oil
4 cans chicken broth (14.5 oz. each)
1/2 cup bamboo shoots, sliced
2 cups green vegetables, such as mustard cabbage,
    watercress, spinach, etc., cut into 2-inch lengths
Salt to taste

Marinate chicken with cornstarch and sesame oil; set aside for 15 minutes. Heat broth until boiling; add chicken and cook for 3 minutes. Skim off froth. Add bamboo shoots and vegetables. Cook until vegetables are done. Taste and add salt, if necessary.

Country Comfort Corn Chowder

yield: 12–14 servings

* *

1/2 pound bacon, chopped
1 medium onion, chopped
1 to 2 stalks celery, chopped
1/4 to 1/2 cup flour
1 quart water (more if necessary)
4 to 5 medium potatoes, diced into chunks
2 cans cream style corn (14.75 oz. each)
Salt and pepper to taste
1 pint half & half
4 tablespoons butter (optional)

Fry bacon until almost done. Add onion and celery; sauté until slightly browned. Gradually blend in flour. Mixture will be thick. Slowly add water and mix until smooth. Add potatoes and bring to a slow boil. Add more water if necessary. Reduce heat and simmer for about 15 to 20 minutes or until potatoes are cooked. Stir occasionally. Add corn and bring to simmer again. Season with salt and pepper and taste; adjust as necessary. Add the half & half and stir until mixed well. Just before serving, add butter, if desired, and stir until melted. Serve immediately.

Variations: Add 1 to 2 cans minced clams; diced shiitake mushrooms, soaked and sliced; diced carrots, etc. or top with seasoned croutons just before serving.

Note: Thanks to Devin Fujioka, who was an eleven-year-old from Kamuela on the Big Island several years ago when he shared this family favorite in his school project cookbook. This corn chowder is so rich and delicious it was brought to my attention as the best! Lisa Fujioka, Devin's mother, created this for those chilly Kamuela nights and named it "Country Comfort Corn Chowder."

Egg Flower Pea Soup

yield: 6 servings

* *

1/2 pound ground pork
2 slices fresh ginger, crushed
5 cups water
1 can peas (17 oz.; *do not drain*)
1 teaspoon salt
1 to 2 eggs, beaten

Brown pork. Add ginger and water. Bring to boil; skim off froth and oil. Lower heat and simmer 20 minutes. Remove ginger slices and add can of peas with liquid and salt. Bring to boil again. Stir in egg. Serve immediately.

Note: This is a variation of an old favorite pea soup that my husband, Don, enjoyed. It had to be canned peas for this soup.

Fu Jook Soup

yield: 10–12 servings

* *

1-1/2 to 2 pounds spare ribs (sweet and sour bone-in type)
4 to 5 dried shiitake mushrooms, soaked and sliced
1 package dried fu jook (dried bean curd) (4 oz.)
1 package long rice (2 oz.)
2-inch piece fresh ginger
1 can chicken broth (14.5 oz.)
Salt to taste

Break fu jook into 2-inch pieces and presoak in cold water for 1 hour. Soak long rice in hot water for 15 minutes. Drain long rice and cut into 3-inch lengths, more or less; set aside.

Place spare ribs in pot; add chicken broth. Add mushrooms, ginger and enough water to cover spare ribs, about 2 inches. Bring to boil and skim off froth. Lower heat; cover and simmer for 1 hour or until meat is tender.

Drain fu jook and add fu jook and long rice to soup. Cook additional half hour. Season with salt.

Variation: If desired, add 4 dried red dates which have been presoaked until softened. Eight dried oysters may also add to the flavor. Sometimes I'll add cut-up squash if available. This is one of our family's "comfort foods." The children like cooked rice in a bowl with this soup poured over for a satisfying meal.

Ga Hap Ca (Steamed Chicken with Tomatoes)

yield: 4 servings

* *

1-1/2 pounds chicken thighs, cut into bite-sized pieces
3 ripe tomatoes, cut into thin wedges
3 stalks green onions, thinly sliced
3 thin slices ginger
1 teaspoon sesame oil
1 teaspoon vegetable oil
2 tablespoons fish sauce
1/2 teaspoon salt
1/2 teaspoon sugar
Black pepper to taste

Place chicken into heatproof bowl. Add rest of ingredients and mix thoroughly. Put the dish in a pan with water to come almost halfway up the dish. Cover and steam for 25 to 35 minutes or until chicken is tender. Stir once or twice. Serve in individual bowls.

Note: While in Hilo, this soup was highly recommended by Roger Pflum. Roger is an avid cook and enjoys trying out new recipes. (He even made joong for the first time for the seniors at Auntie Sally's for Chinese New Year. It was delicious!)

Note: I use a 10 cup Pyrex® bowl placed in a large wide pot. The chicken is especially tender because it is steamed. The liquid for soup accumulates as it is being steamed.

Hearty Miso Soup

yield: 6 servings

* *

2 tablespoons small iriko
4 cups water
1/2 cup round onion, chopped
1 potato, peeled, cut in half lengthwise and
    then cut into 1/4-inch slices
1/4 block kamaboko, cut into strips
1 aburage, cut into strips
1 ounce somen (a small handful), soaked and
    cut into shorter lengths
4 to 5 tablespoons miso, blended with a little water
1/4 cup green onion, chopped for garnish

Combine first three ingredients and simmer, covered, about 15 minutes. Add potato, kamaboko, aburage and somen; simmer another 6 to 8 minutes. Stir in blended miso; simmer a minute and serve in individual bowls. Sprinkle green onion on top, if desired.

Note: I met my good friend, Eleanor Tokunaga, at the supermarket one day and asked her for her favorite soup recipe. I jotted down her recipe for her hearty miso soup which she calls "a meal in itself." She also substitutes udon noodles for the somen if she has some udon available. If she has gobo, she'll put that in, too.

Hot and Sour Thai Soup

yield: 4 servings

* *

**4 chicken thighs, boneless and skinless
(or 12-oz. chicken breast)
4 stalks lemongrass
2 limes
2 cans chicken broth (14.5 oz. each)
1/2 cup water
4 slices fresh ginger
1 teaspoon brown sugar
3 tablespoons shallots, minced
2 tablespoons fish sauce
2 teaspoons chili garlic sauce (or more to taste)
2 tablespoons Chinese parsley, chopped**

Prepare lemongrass. Use only bottom 5 inches of lemongrass and discard rest. Place 8 to 10 outside sheaths into medium soup pot. Mince the bottom 2 inches of the tender inside leaves and set aside 2 to 3 tablespoons.

With a potato peeler, peel 6 strips of rind from one lime (or substitute 2 to 3 Kaffir lime leaves if available) and place in pot. Place broth, water, chicken, ginger and brown sugar in same pot and bring to boil. Lower heat to simmer. Cover and cook for 15 minutes at an active simmer.

Grate rind of remaining lime to measure 1/4 to 1/2 teaspoon and set aside. Juice both limes to measure out 3 tablespoons juice; set aside.

When chicken is cooked, remove from broth and shred with 2 forks. Strain broth of any solids. Place broth back into pot.

(continued on next page)

Add chicken, minced lemongrass, grated lime rind and juice, shallots, fish sauce and garlic chili pepper sauce. Bring back to simmer and sprinkle with Chinese parsley. Serve immediately.

Note: When peeling or grating lime, be sure to use only the outer green rind. The inside white part is bitter tasting. Peeling a lime is not so easy. Get a firm grip and use a slow back and forth motion to carefully peel off a strip.

Hot and Sour Soup
yield: 4 servings

✳ ✳

2 cans chicken broth (14.5 oz. each) or 4 cups chicken broth
1/4 cup lean pork or chicken, cut into strips
2 tablespoons bamboo shoots, julienned
1 tablespoon black fungus, softened in water and julienned
2 tablespoons soy sauce
1/2 teaspoon pepper (or less, adjust to taste)
3 tablespoons cornstarch blended with 3 tablespoons water
2 eggs, lightly beaten
2 tablespoons vinegar
1 teaspoon sesame oil
2 teaspoons green onions, thinly sliced

Heat chicken broth; add pork or chicken, bamboo shoots and black fungus. Bring to boil; add soy sauce and pepper. Lower heat and simmer 2 to 3 minutes. Then while soup is simmering, stir in cornstarch and water mixture, making certain that it is mixed in evenly. Steadily stir eggs and vinegar into soup in a steady stream; simmer 1 to 2 minutes. Add sesame oil and green onions just before serving.

Note: Very quick and simple to prepare and very tasty. I lessen the amount of pepper, but that's a matter of preference.

Jook (Chinese Rice Soup)

yield: 6–8 servings

* *

Chicken or turkey bones
1 cup uncooked rice
1 teaspoon salt
1/2 teaspoon sherry
1/2 teaspoon oil
2 tablespoons chung choi, rinsed and minced

Condiments:

Iceberg lettuce leaves, shredded
Green onions, thinly sliced
Soy sauce and pepper to taste
Chinese parsley, chopped (optional)
"1,000-year-old" eggs, chopped (optional)
Fried wun tun strips (optional)

In large pot, place chicken or turkey bones and cover with water; bring to boil and simmer about 1 to 1-1/2 hours. Cool and strain broth to remove bones. Shred any meat off bones; set aside. Add enough water to broth to measure 11 cups liquid and pour back into pot.

Rinse rice until water is clear. Cover rice with warm water and stir in salt, sherry and oil. Let sit for 15 minutes.

Bring broth to boil and add rice with liquid, chung choi and any shredded meat. Simmer about 1 hour at somewhere between medium and medium–low heat with cover slightly ajar. Stir occasionally and adjust heat as necessary. Add more water if needed. (Be careful of jook spilling over or sticking to pot.)

Serve jook in bowls and provide condiments for garnish.

(continued on next page)

Provide soy sauce and pepper also.

Note: My husband, Don, likes chicken liver in jook. I boil chicken livers separately and cut into slices. Just before serving, I add a portion serving of liver into the jook for him, heat and serve.

....

Imitation Bird Nest Soup
yield: 5–6 servings

* *

1 bundle long rice (2 oz.), soaked in hot water for 1 hour
4 shiitake mushrooms, soaked in water to soften
1 cup bamboo shoots, thinly sliced
3 cans chicken broth (14.5 oz. each)
1/2 cup pork, thinly sliced
1/2 cup ham, thinly sliced
2 eggs, beaten
1/2 cup green onions, thinly sliced

Drain long rice and cut into approximately 1/4-inch pieces. Drain mushrooms; discard stems and slice mushrooms into thin strips. Combine long rice, mushrooms, bamboo shoots and broth; bring to boil. Add pork and ham; simmer for 15 to 20 minutes. Just before serving, stir in beaten eggs and green onions.

Variation: Substitute green onions with Chinese parsley. Substitute bamboo shoots with 1/2 cup chopped water chestnuts.

Kim Chee Miso Soup

yield: 4 servings

* *

1/4 pound lean pork, cut into slivers (about 1/4 cup)
1 teaspoon fresh ginger, slivered
2 teaspoons oil
3 cups water
1 small potato, sliced and cut into bite-sized pieces
1 small carrot, sliced
1/2 cup daikon, cut into strips
1/4 cup green onions, chopped
1/2 to 1 cup kim chee, chopped
1 to 2 tablespoons miso, blended with a little water

Heat oil and stir-fry pork and ginger. Add water and bring to boil; simmer for 2 to 3 minutes. Add potato, carrot, daikon and green onions. Simmer 8 to 10 minutes or until vegetables are tender. Add kim chee and stir in miso. Simmer an additional 1 to 2 minutes.

Note: Lots of vegetables in this miso soup. Begin with 1/2 cup kim chee and add more to your taste. Surprisingly, potato slices taste great in miso soup and give it body.

Kim Chee Soup

yield: 4 servings

* *

8 to 10 ounces ground pork or thinly sliced lean pork
3 slices fresh ginger
3 cans chicken broth (14.5 oz. each)
1 jar kim chee (12 oz., e.g., Kohala
    Won-Bok® Kim Chee), include liquid
1-1/2 pounds wintermelon or long squash,
    cut into 1-1/2 x 2-1/2-inch pieces (about 15)
1 block firm tofu (20 oz.), cut into 1-inch cubes

Brown ground pork with ginger; drain oil. Add chicken broth. Chop kim chee into smaller pieces and, together with kim chee liquid, add to soup. Add wintermelon or long squash and simmer for 15 to 20 minutes or until wintermelon or long squash becomes soft. Add tofu and cook about 1 to 2 minutes more.

Note: Lessen amount if kim chee is too hot for your taste.

Lentil and Brown Rice Soup

yield: 6 servings

* *

1 envelope Lipton® Onion Soup mix
4 cups water
3/4 cup lentils, rinsed
1/2 cup uncooked brown rice (or white rice), rinsed
1 can whole peeled tomatoes (14 oz.),
    drained and coarsely chopped (reserve liquid)
1 carrot, chopped
1 stalk celery, chopped
1/2 teaspoon basil leaves
1/4 teaspoon thyme leaves
1/4 teaspoon oregano
1 tablespoon fresh parsley, finely chopped
1 tablespoon apple cider vinegar
1/4 teaspoon pepper
Tabasco® sauce to taste (optional)

In large pot, combine onion soup mix, water, lentils, rice, tomatoes and reserved liquid, carrot, celery, basil, thyme and oregano. Bring to boil, then simmer, covered, for 45 minutes or until lentils and rice are tender; stir occasionally. Add remaining ingredients; stir and simmer 5 minutes longer.

Note: A hearty and healthy soup. Add more water to thin soup, if desired.

Minestrone Soup
yield: 12–14 servings

* *

1 can condensed beef consommé soup (10.5 oz.)
2 teaspoons instant beef bouillon or 2 bouillon cubes
5 cups water
1 large onion, finely chopped
1 clove garlic, minced
3 tablespoons fresh parsley, chopped, or 1 tablespoon dry
2 carrots, shredded or finely chopped
2 stalks celery with leaves, diced
1 large potato, diced
1-1/4 teaspoons Italian seasoning

Combine all ingredients above; boil 1 minute. Lower heat, cover and simmer 30 minutes, stirring occasionally.

1 pound ground beef, cooked and drained
1 cup macaroni, uncooked
1 can tomatoes with liquid (28 oz.), do not drain, but chop
   tomatoes into smaller pieces
1 teaspoon salt
1/4 teaspoon pepper
1 can kidney beans (15 oz.), with liquid

Add remaining ingredients and simmer additional 20 minutes.

Optional: Serve with a sprinkle of parmesan cheese, if desired.

Note: Mary Alice Clark gave me this fantastic minestrone soup recipe. It's easier to make than it appears and it's so-o-o good. Many others enjoyed it so much that Mary Alice used to make this soup as a Christmas gift to her friends and neighbors.

Miso Soup

yield: 6–8 servings

* *

6 cups water
1/2 cup dried shrimp
1/2 cup miso, blended with 1/4 cup water
1 block tofu (14 oz.), cut into cubes
1/4 cup green onions, thinly sliced (for garnish)

Boil shrimp in water for 20 minutes. Strain and discard shrimp. Bring shrimp-flavored water to boil again. Add blended miso and simmer 10 to 15 minutes. Add tofu; cook until tofu is heated through. Serve in soup bowls and garnish with green onions.

Note: This is a favorite soup of my grandchildren. Whenever their mother serves salmon for dinner, she also prepares this simple soup to go with the meal. Feeling under the weather? Miso soup is great!

Miso Soup with Mixed Vegetables

yield: 6−8 servings

* *

6 cups water
1 tablespoon dried shrimp
1 packet bonito flavored soup base (no MSG)
1/2 cup miso, blended with 1/4 cup water
1 package frozen "Boiled Mixed Vegetables" (10.5 oz.),
    Shirakiku® brand
1 carrot, sliced
2 to 3 Chinese cabbage leaves, chopped
1/4 cup green onions, thinly sliced (for garnish)

Boil shrimp in water for 20 minutes; add 1 packet soup base. Stir in blended miso. Add frozen vegetables, carrot and Chinese cabbage and simmer 10 to 15 minutes or until vegetables are tender. Serve in soup bowls and garnish with green onions.

Note: Everyone has his favorite recipes and I enjoy learning about what others like. So when I met David Lung, I asked him about his favorite soup. He said he likes the miso soup with nishime vegetables that his daughter-in-law prepares. That sounded interesting and since I like nishime, I put together this recipe using frozen nishime vegetables to make it easier for a busy homemaker. It is very tasty!

Variation: Add other vegetables such as shiitake mushrooms, lotus root, bamboo shoots, etc.

Noodles and Vegetables in Broth

yield: 6 servings

* *

8 ounces wide egg noodles (or linguine, vermicelli, etc.)
6 cups chicken broth
2 cups cooked chicken, cubed
1 carrot, cut into thin diagonal slices
1 stalk celery, cut into thin diagonal slices
1/2 cup Chinese cabbage, thinly sliced
2 stalks green onions, cut in half lengthwise,
    then in 1-inch pieces
1 tablespoon soy sauce
White pepper to taste

Cook noodles according to package directions; drain and set aside. Heat chicken broth and add rest of ingredients (except noodles). Simmer about 5 to 10 minutes or until vegetables are just barely cooked. Divide noodles among 6 soup bowls; pour vegetable broth over. Serve immediately.

Ong Choy and Pork Soup

yield: 6–8 servings

* *

4 cans chicken broth (14.5 oz. each)
1/4 pound lean pork, slivered
2 pieces shiitake mushroom, soaked and sliced
1 slice ginger (about 3/4-inch length)
1/4 cup celery, thinly sliced diagonally
1/4 cup green onions, cut into 1-inch lengths
1 bunch ong choy, cut into 2-inch lengths
1/4 cup raw shrimp, peeled and deveined,
    cut into bite-sized pieces
Salt and pepper to taste

Bring chicken broth to boil and add mushrooms, pork, ginger, celery and green onions. Reduce heat and simmer, covered, for 10 to 15 minutes. Add ong choy and simmer about 3 minutes, or until ong choy is cooked. Stir in shrimp. Season with salt and pepper to taste.

Pho

yield: 4 servings

* *

1 package rice sticks (8 oz.)
2 stalks green onions, thinly sliced
6 to 8 ounces sirloin, partially frozen and thinly sliced

Broth:

5 cups beef stock or 3 cans lower sodium
    beef broth (14 oz. each)
1 inch fresh ginger
3 star anise
2 stalks green onions, chopped
3 tablespoons fish sauce

Garnish:

2 cups mung bean sprouts
12 fresh basil leaves (Thai)
mint leaves
1 lime, quartered
Hoisin sauce, to taste (optional)
Hot chili sauce, to taste (optional)
2 jalapeno or serrano chilies, thinly sliced

Soak rice sticks in warm water for 30 minutes. Prepare broth. Combine beef stock, ginger, star anise, green onions and fish sauce; gently simmer for 30 minutes. Strain stock; set aside. Prepare garnish on platter; set aside.

Just before serving, bring 4 quarts water to boil. (Also bring broth to boil so broth is boiling about the same time as rice

(continued on next page)

sticks are done.) Drain soaking rice sticks; place in boiling water and cook for 30 seconds. Drain and divide the noodles among 4 large bowls. Arrange beef slices and green onions on top.

Spoon the boiling broth on top. (The hot broth should be sufficient to cook the meat.) Serve immediately. Let each person add sprouts, mint, basil leaves, etc., from the garnish platter.

'Ono Hamburger Soup
yield: 6 servings

3/4 to 1 pound ground beef, browned and drained
1 quart water
3 beef bouillon cubes
1 onion, chopped
1 can whole peeled tomatoes (14-1/4 oz.); Do not drain, but chop tomatoes into smaller pieces.
1 can tomato soup (10-3/4 oz.)
1 stalk celery, chopped
2 small carrots, cubed
2 tablespoons uncooked rice
1 teaspoon dried parsley flakes

In large pot combine water, ground beef, bouillon cubes and onion; bring to boil. Skim off oil. Add rest of ingredients and simmer for 1-1/2 to 2 hours, stirring occasionally.

Ozoni

yield: 6–8 servings

* *

8 cups water
1/2 cup dried shrimp
3 to 4 shiitake mushrooms, soaked and thinly sliced
1/4 cup gobo, scraped clean and slivered (Soak in water
    to prevent discoloration)
1/4 cup carrot, slivered
2 strips nishime konbu, washed and tied in knots about
    2 inches apart, cut between knots
2 cups mizuna, cut into 1-inch lengths
2 tablespoons soy sauce
1 teaspoon salt
1 block kamaboko (6 oz.), sliced
Mochi, whole or small pieces, enough for 6 to 8 servings

Place shrimp in cold water. Bring to boil and simmer over medium–low heat for 20 to 25 minutes. Strain. Place broth back on stove and discard shrimp. Add sliced mushroom, gobo, carrot and konbu. Simmer until vegetables are tender (about 5 to 10 minutes). Add mizuna. Add soy sauce and salt to taste. Simmer and place some mochi pieces into pot and cook just until mochi is heated and softened to your taste. Place heated mochi and 2 to 3 kamaboko slices into soup bowl and ladle soup liquid over. (Only heat enough mochi for desired amount of servings.)

Oxtail Soup

yield: 4–6 servings

* *

4 pounds oxtail, cut into pieces
2 cubes beef bouillon (Knorr® brand, Extra Large Cubes)
2 cubes chicken bouillon (Knorr® brand, Extra Large Cubes)
5 whole star anise
4 slivers ginger
1 cup raw peanuts, shelled and skinned
Hawaiian salt to taste
Chinese parsley for garnish

Parboil oxtail 20 to 30 minutes. Rinse and trim fat. Place in pot and cover with water approximately 2 inches above oxtail. Bring to boil and add bouillon cubes, star anise and ginger. Simmer for 1 hour. Add peanuts. Simmer for another 1 to 1-1/2 hours, or until oxtail is tender. Skim off "scum" from broth. Add Hawaiian salt to taste. Garnish with Chinese parsley.

Variation: Serve with ground ginger and soy sauce as a condiment. Serve with cooked vegetables such as mustard cabbage and Chinese cabbage that can be added to soup if desired.

Note: Soak raw shelled peanuts in warm water to easily remove skin.

Pork and Mustard Cabbage Soup

yield: 4 servings

* *

1/2 cup lean pork, thinly sliced
2 teaspoons oil
Sprinkle Hawaiian salt and pepper to taste
2 cans chicken broth (14.5 oz. each)
1/2 cup water
1/2 pound mustard cabbage, chopped into 1-inch pieces

Season pork slices with a light sprinkle of Hawaiian salt and pepper. Heat oil and pork; fry until lightly browned. Add chicken broth and water. Bring to boil, lower heat and simmer about 15 minutes. Add mustard cabbage and simmer, uncovered, until tender (about 7 minutes).

Note: Here is a soup that will have your keiki enjoy mustard cabbage! Glennis Ooka often prepares this soup for her preschool twins who will heartily eat this for dinner. She suggests adding a little cooked rice in a bowl and pouring the soup over and it's a meal. My granddaughter, Kristen, who resists eating anything green, will eat the mustard cabbage if it is cooked this way.

Pork and Squash Soup with Miso

yield: 3–4 servings

✳ ✳

1 pound spareribs (or pork bones)
2 cans chicken broth (14.5 oz. each)
1-1/2 to 2 pounds long squash
1 package nishime konbu (1 oz.) (optional)
1 tablespoon soy sauce
2 tablespoons miso, blended with a little water
2 leaves Chinese cabbage, chopped (optional)

If using nishime konbu, rinse konbu and lightly tie into knots. Cut between knots and set aside.

Parboil spareribs in boiling water; boil vigorously for 1 to 2 minutes. Drain and rinse ribs with water, removing any scum on spare ribs. Lightly scrub same pot to remove any scum inside pot. Place spareribs back in pan; add chicken broth and 1 cup water. Add nishime konbu, if desired. Bring to boil, lower heat and cook uncovered for about 50 minutes.

Peel squash and cut into thick slices. (If squash seeds are matured and hard, discard seeds.) Add squash to soup and simmer 15 minutes more. When squash is tender, add soy sauce and miso; heat 10 more minutes. If desired, add Chinese cabbage just before serving.

Note: An old Okinawan soup recipe with lots of flavor. Sayoko Watanabe almost always has soup with her supper and seldom uses recipes. I had to watch her one day as she prepared this soup so I could measure and write the directions.

Variation: Daikon may be used in place of squash.

Portuguese Bean Soup

yield: 8–10 servings

* *

1 to 2 pounds ham shank (or ham hock)
3 cans chicken broth (14.5 oz. each)
2 cans kidney beans (15 oz. each)
2 cans tomato sauce (8 oz. each)
1 clove garlic, crushed
1 teaspoon pepper
1 medium onion, chopped
4 potatoes, cubed into 1-1/2-inch pieces
4 carrots, cut into 1-1/2-inch pieces
1 Portuguese sausage (10 oz.), cut into 1/2-inch slices
1 bay leaf
1 small head cabbage

In large pot, cover ham shank with chicken broth. Add enough water to cover and boil until tender (about 1 to 2 hours). Skim off fat while cooking. Add rest of ingredients and cook until tender. Continue to skim off fat.

Note: This is my all-time favorite Portuguese Bean Soup. It is *so* delicious! You can prepare this a day or two ahead and just heat it up for a quick meal.

Quick Corn Chowder

yield: 6 servings

❋ ❋

6 slices bacon, chopped
1/2 onion, chopped
1 potato, diced
1/2 cup water
1 can whole kernal corn (11 oz.)
2 cups milk
Salt and pepper to taste
1 tablespoon flour mixed with 1 tablespoon water

In medium pot, cook bacon until browned. Drain half of fat. Add onion; cook until soft. Add potato and stir-fry with onion for a few minutes. Add water and corn. Cover and simmer, stirring occasionaly, until potatoes are soft, about 10 to 15 minutes. Add milk; cook 5 minutes or until milk is heated. Add salt and pepper. Thicken soup with blended flour and water.

Note: This is a family favorite and one I especially like because it is so easy and quick to prepare.

Variation: Add 1 can Snow's® New England Clam Chowder (10-3/4-oz.) and blend into soup.

Scallop Soup

yield: 6 servings

* *

20 dried scallops
8 cups water
1 can bamboo shoots already cut into thin strips (15 oz.),
  drained
Salt to taste
4 tablespoons cornstarch blended with 8 tablespoons water
2 eggs, beaten

Lightly rinse dried scallops to remove white film on surface. Place in saucepan with water. Bring to boil; simmer 1-1/2 to 2 hours or until scallops are soft. Skim off white foam. Transfer scallops to a bowl leaving liquid in saucepan. Add more water to measure 8 cups liquid.

Shred scallops and discard hard muscles, if necessary. Place shredded scallops back into saucepan and reheat. Add bamboo shoots and salt to taste. Thicken with cornstarch and water. Pour beaten egg over the back of a fork and stir in circular motion so that egg does not clump together. Cook 1 minute more.

Note: A great tasting soup with lots of shredded scallops in every bowl! Edward Au has shared another great recipe with us.

Variation: It's not necessary, but, just before serving, you may want to garnish with a little chopped Chinese parsley or some slivered ham.

Seafood Bisque

yield: 4–6 servings

* *

2 tablespoons butter
2 cloves garlic, minced
3 stalks celery, minced
2 cans cream of celery soup (10.7 oz. each)
5 cans water (use soup can)
1 pound fish, cut in 1-inch pieces (e.g., mahimahi and cod)
12 clams in shell, rinsed
1/2 pound shrimp, shell on (51 to 60 count)
1 tablespoon parsley, chopped (or parsley flakes)
Salt and pepper to taste

Melt butter in large pot; add garlic and celery and sauté. Add cream of celery soup and water. Bring to boil. Add fish; cook for 5 minutes. Lower heat; add clams and shrimp. Cover and simmer for 10 to 15 minutes. Add parsley. Season with salt and pepper.

Note: Tastes great with garlic bread. Scallop and crab may be substituted.

Seaweed Soup

yield: 6 servings

* *

1/2 pound lean pork, thinly sliced
1/3 cup fueru wakame, soaked
6 cups water
1 small carrot, sliced
8 water chestnuts, sliced
1 teaspoon salt
Dash pepper
2 mustard leaves, cut into 1-1/2-inch lengths

Marinade:

2 teaspoons cornstarch
1 teaspoon sugar
1/4 teaspoon pepper
4 teaspoons soy sauce

Marinate pork at least 15 minutes. Set aside.

Squeeze wakame to remove all liquid. Bring water to boil; add pork and simmer 5 minutes. Skim off "scum." Stir in wakame, carrot, water chestnuts, salt and pepper. Simmer for 3 minutes. Add mustard leaves; simmer 2 more minutes or until mustard cabbage is done to your taste.

Squash Soup

yield: 4–6 servings

* *

1/2 medium wintermelon or long squash,
   peeled and cubed
2 to 3 cans chicken broth (14.5 oz. each)
1 can water (use soup can)
2 packages long rice (2 oz. each), soaked,
   drained and cut into 3-inch lengths
1 tablespoon sambal oelek, adjust to taste
1 tablespoon vinegar
1 packet bonito-flavored soup base
3 medium shiitake mushrooms, soaked and sliced
1 tablespoon wakame
1 tablespoon fresh ginger, chopped (optional)
1/4 cup soy sauce, adjust to taste
2 tablespoons sugar

Mix all in pot and bring to boil about 25 minutes on medium heat. Lower heat and simmer another 15 minutes.

Note: Gene Yoshinaga grew his own winter melon and prepared this squash soup from a recipe which he altered and refined. Wintermelon is not often found at the supermarket so I really appreciated Gene not only sharing his recipe with me but providing me with the winter melon to cook the soup.

Variation: Gene suggests adding cubed tofu or shredded chicken to the soup.

Turkey Chowder

yield: 2–3 servings

* *

1 strip bacon, chopped
1/4 cup onion, diced
2 stalks celery, diced
1 large potato, cubed
1 cup cooked turkey, diced
2 cups turkey broth or 1 can chicken broth (14.5 oz.)
1 can whole kernal corn (11 oz.)
2 tablespoons fresh parsley, chopped
2 tablespoons flour
1 cup milk
Salt and pepper to taste

In medium saucepan, fry bacon pieces until crispy; drain, reserving about 2 tablespoons bacon drippings. Add onion and celery to bacon and drippings. Cook until soft. Add broth (if using 1 can chicken broth, add enough water to make 2 cups). Heat to boiling and add potatoes and turkey. Simmer until potatoes are tender. Add corn and parsley. Blend flour with milk and stir into cooking mixture. Cook about 15 minutes longer, stirring occasionally.

Note: It's a great way to use leftover turkey after Thanksgiving.

Vegetable Soup

yield: 6 – 8 servings

* *

5 cups total combination of any fresh vegetables (e.g., carrots, potatoes, onion, green beans, celery, zucchini, cabbage, etc.), except tomatoes
1 can diced tomatoes (14.5 oz.)
2 cans vegetable broth (14 oz. each)
1 cup water
1/2 teaspoon each of various dried herbs (e.g., basil, oregano, thyme, rosemary, etc.)
1/2 teaspoon salt
1/4 teaspoon pepper

Combine all ingredients in large pot; bring to boil. Stir soup and lower heat. Cover and simmer 50 minutes, or until all vegetables are tender. (Simmer another hour or longer for better flavor.)

Note: A great way to clean out your refrigerator and get a great tasting soup at the same time. My husband, Don, loves to do this. When he does, he adds more water, more vegetables, a packet of instant onion soup mix and a dash of Tabasco® for more flavor. Be creative!

Vegetable Soup with Spinach

yield: 6 servings

* *

Stock:

3-1/2 to 4 pounds chicken or 8 chicken thighs
2 quarts water
1 onion, coarsely chopped
1 leek, coarsely chopped and rinsed
1 carrot, coarsely chopped
1 tomato, quartered
2 cloves garlic, smashed
1 bay leaf
2 sprigs fresh thyme
4 sprigs American parsley
8 black peppercorns

Cut chicken into 9 pieces. Discard skin and cut away any large pieces of fat. If using thighs, remove skin and excess fat. In large pot, combine all ingredients and bring to boil. Lower heat and simmer with the cover ajar for 40 minutes, adjusting heat to maintain a simmer. Strain stock through a triple layer of cheesecloth. Reserve chicken for another use. Chill stock overnight and remove the layer of fat that forms.

(continued on next page)

Soup:

2 red potatoes, cut into 3/4-inch chunks
Salt and black pepper
2 leeks, white and light-green part only, cut into half lengthwise
    and then into 1/2-inch slices, and rinsed well
2 carrots, sliced
1 cup frozen peas
2 cups baby spinach
2 tablespoons American parsley, chopped

Bring stock to simmer in large saucepan over medium heat. Add potatoes and 1/2 teaspoon salt; simmer 5 minutes. Add leeks and carrots and simmer 5 minutes more or until vegetables are tender. Add peas, spinach and parsley and cook for 1 minute. Season with salt and pepper.

Watercress Egg-Drop Soup
yield: 4 servings

* *

2 cans chicken broth (14.5 oz. each)
1 clove garlic, lightly crushed
2 thin slices fresh ginger
1 bunch watercress, coarsely chopped into about
    1-1/2-inch lengths
1 egg, lightly beaten

Combine first 3 ingredients in medium saucepan; bring to boil. Add watercress and simmer until softened. Add egg, stirring, until egg is lightly cooked. Remove garlic and ginger slices. Serve immediately.

Vegetarian Corn Chowder

yield: 6 – 8 servings

* *

1 large potato, peeled and cubed (about 2 cups)
2 cups water
1 teaspoon salt
1/2 teaspoon celery salt
1/2 teaspoon parsley flakes
1-1/2 stalks celery, diced (about 1 cup)
1/2 cup onion, chopped
1 bay leaf
1 can cream-style corn (14.75 oz.)
1 can corn niblets (11 oz.)
2 cups soy milk (more or less)

Place all ingredients (except last 3) in large pot; simmer over low heat until potatoes are almost done (about 5 to 10 minutes). Stir in niblets and cream-style corn and simmer 10 minutes, stirring frequently. Add soy milk to desired consistency. Turn heat off and let stand 15 to 20 minutes. Remove bay leaf before serving.

Note: I had never used soy milk until Nancy Ishikawa gave me this recipe. Not only is this soup very delicious but I also learned to use and enjoy soy milk in place of my Lactaid® milk.

Vegetarian Portuguese Bean Soup

yield: 8 –10 servings

* *

8 oz. dry red kidney beans (half of 16-oz. package),
    soaked overnight
2 quarts water
3 extra large bouillon cubes, beef or chicken
1 can tomato sauce (8 oz.)
1 onion, chopped
3 to 4 carrots, chopped
2 potatoes, chopped
1/4 head cabbage, chopped
Hawaiian salt to taste
Pepper to taste
Pinch cinnamon
1 tablespoon parsley flakes
2 to 3 cups watercress, chopped

Drain beans. Bring 2 quarts water to boil. Add beans, bouillon cubes, tomato sauce and onions and simmer for 1-1/2 hours, or until beans are tender. Add carrots; cook for 15 minutes. Add potatoes and rest of ingredients; simmer for another 20 minutes or until potatoes are cooked.

Note: Betty Kaniaupio prepares this Portuguese Bean Soup version for her daughter and others who are vegetarians. The pinch of cinnamon is the secret ingredient tip from her mother which gives the soup a special flavor. I recommend this soup to non-vegetarians also. It is very tasty and filling.

Won Ton Soup

yield: 5–6 servings

* *

2 packages won ton wrappers (12 oz. each)
4 cans chicken broth (14-1/2 oz. each)
Chinese parsley or green onions, chopped,
    for garnish (optional)
3 quarts water

Filling:

1 pound ground pork
1/2 pound shrimp, cleaned and chopped
1/2 cup water chestnuts, finely minced
1 teaspoon Hawaiian salt
1 teaspoon sesame oil
1 teaspoon soy sauce
1/2 teaspoon cornstarch
1/2 teaspoon sugar
1/2 teaspoon oyster sauce

Combine filling ingredients and mix well. Place about 1 teaspoon of pork filling on won ton wrapper. Wet edges and fold into a triangle. Wet left side of won ton skin. Pull sides back and pinch together, placing one side on top of the sealer.

Boil 3 quarts water rapidly. Place 10 won tons into boiling water. Won tons are cooked when they float to the top. Test for doneness. More filling may require more cooking time. Repeat procedure until all are cooked. Rinse in cold water as they are removed. Drain and place in soup bowls. Pour desired amount of heated chicken broth over won tons. Garnish with Chinese parsley or green onions, if desired.

Salads

Ambrosia

yield: 12 – 16 servings

* *

1 container cottage cheese, fat free and
    small curd (16 oz.)
1 container light Cool Whip® (8 oz.)
1 box instant vanilla pudding (3.4 oz.)
2 cans mandarin oranges (11 oz. each), drained
2 cans fruit cocktail, light syrup
    (15-1/4 oz. each), drained
2 cans peaches, light syrup (15-1/4 oz. each), drained
2 cans pineapple chunks in own juices
    (15-1/4 oz. each), drained

Mix together cottage cheese, Cool Whip® and pudding. Pour
fruits into cottage cheese mixture and mix well.

Easy Chicken Salad

yield: 10 – 12 servings

* *

1 head iceberg lettuce, torn into bite-sized pieces
1 bunch radish sprouts (6 oz.), trim bottoms
3 skinless and boneless chicken thighs, cooked
    in slightly salted water and shredded
1 cucumber, seeded and thinly sliced
1/2 head purple cabbage, thinly sliced
6 ounces sliced almonds, toasted
1 bottle Italian dressing (16 oz.), or any favorite
    dressing of your choice

Toss all ingredients together (except dressing). Refrigerate.
Add desired amount of dressing just before serving.

Arrowhead Salad

yield: 8–10 servings

* *

1 head cabbage, thinly sliced
1 package frozen peas (10 oz.), parboiled
1 package slivered almonds (2 oz.), or shelled
    roasted pine nuts
3 chicken breasts, cooked and diced
2 stalks green onions, chopped
1 package Ichiban® packaged dry saimin (3.5 oz.),
    broken in pieces

Dressing:

1 package dashi from noodle package
1/3 cup sugar
2/3 cup salad oil
1 teaspoon salt
Pinch pepper
6 tablespoons Japanese vinegar

Combine dressing ingredients. Combine salad ingredients and pour dressing on just prior to serving.

Auntie Betty's Famous
Potato Salad

yield: 12–14 servings

* *

4 russet potatoes, boiled and cut into 1-inch cubes
2 cups salad macaroni, follow directions on package but
    do not rinse with water after cooking
1/2 cup frozen peas and carrots, boil 3 to 5 minutes
    or until tender, drain
4 hardboiled eggs, chopped
1/4 cup onion, diced (optional)
8 ounces imitation crab, shredded
Mayonnaise (Best Foods® brand recommended)
Salt and pepper to taste

Mix all ingredients except mayonnaise, salt and pepper. Refrigerate overnight. Add desired amount of mayonnaise, salt and pepper to taste. Refrigerate.

Cauliflower and Broccoli Salad

yield: 8 servings

* *

1 head cauliflower, cut into bite-sized pieces
1 stalk broccoli, cut into bite-sized pieces
1 can crabmeat (6 oz.), shredded
2 eggs, hardboiled and sliced
2/3 cup mayonnaise
Dash salt

Parboil cauliflower and broccoli separately; rinse in cold water. Drain well. In large bowl, combine vegetables, crab and eggs; toss. Add mayonnaise and salt; mix together. Refrigerate.

Pasta Salad

* *

1 pound pasta noodles (e.g., Tricolor Fusilli Springs rotini),
    cook according to package directions
2 to 3 bell peppers (green, red or yellow), chopped
2 to 3 tomatoes, cut
1 can small pitted olives (6 oz.), drained
1 cup red onion, chopped
1 can kidney beans (15.5 oz.), drained
1/4 cup dried basil leaves (optional)
1 cup Italian dressing (e.g., Bernstein's® Italian Dressing);
    add more to taste
Salt and pepper to taste

Put cooked noodles in large bowl. Add chopped vegetables.
Begin with 1 cup Italian dressing and add more to taste.
Season with salt, pepper and basil. Chill and serve.

Note: This is a great potluck! Michelle Tobias prepared this
tasty and colorful pasta salad for a baby shower luncheon and
we all enjoyed it.

Bean Salad

yield: 8–10 servings

* *

3 or more kinds of canned beans (green, yellow wax,
    kidney, soy, and garbanzo), drained well
1 medium Maui onion, thinly sliced
1 can whole mushrooms (6.5 oz.), drained
1 green pepper, sliced (optional)
1 can baby corn, whole spears (15 oz.) (optional)

Marinade:

1/4 cup sugar
2/3 cup vinegar
1/3 cup Wesson® oil
1 teaspoon salt

Marinate ingredients in marinade. Best if prepared a day or more before serving.

Note: Here is another "oldie but goodie" recipe from my Puohala Elementary School days in the 1970s. Thanks to Ethel Nishida who shared this recipe with us. I still make it, Ethel!

BLT Salad

yield: 4 servings

* *

1 head iceberg lettuce
6 slices bacon
2 tomatoes
1/3 cup mayonnaise
1/4 teaspoon salt (adjust to taste)
1/4 teaspoon cayenne pepper

Chop or tear lettuce into bite-sized pieces; cover and refrigerate until ready to serve.

Seed tomatoes by cutting them in half and squeezing over sink to get rid of most of the seeds. Chop the tomatoes into 1-inch pieces. Place in bowl and add mayonnaise, salt and pepper. Cover and chill at least 30 minutes.

Cook bacon until crisp; drain on paper towels. Chop and set aside.

When ready to serve, combine lettuce, bacon and tomatoes. Toss to coat evenly.

Note: If you like BLT sandwiches, you'll like this salad.

Broccoli Salad

* *

3 to 4 cups broccoli (raw or blanched), cut into
   bite-sized pieces
1 small carrot, shredded
1/4 cup Maui onion or red onion, chopped
1/4 cup raisins, plumped in water and drained
6 strips bacon, cooked crisp and crumbled (for garnish)

Dressing:

1/2 cup mayonnaise
1/8 cup sugar
2 tablespoons apple cider vinegar

Combine broccoli, carrot, onions and raisins; chill. Blend together dressing ingredients and chill. Just before serving, toss together broccoli mix and desired amount of dressing. Garnish with crumbled bacon.

Broccoli Salad Supreme

yield: 4–6 servings as a side dish

* *

**2 bunches broccoli flowerettes, cut into bite-sized
    pieces (blanch, if desired)
2 tablespoons green onion, thinly sliced
1/3 cup salted sunflower seeds
1/4 cup raisins
Bacon bits or crisped crumbled bacon for garnish (optional)**

Dressing:

**3 tablespoons sugar
1 tablespoon vinegar
1/2 cup mayonnaise**

Mix mayonnaise, sugar and vinegar. Pour over broccoli,
green onion, seeds and raisins. Mix well. Refrigerate to chill.
Crisped crumbled bacon may be added before serving.

Broccoli Shrimp Salad

yield: 8 –10 servings

* *

3 broccoli crowns (1-1/2 to 2 pounds), cut into
    bite-sized pieces and blanched
3/4 pound shrimp, cleaned and boiled
1/2 can whole olives (half of 6 oz. can), drained
2 jars marinated artichoke hearts (6.5 oz. each), drained
1 yellow bell pepper, diced into 1/2-inch squares
6 fresh mushrooms, quartered
6 cocktail tomatoes, cut in fourths or 12 grape tomatoes,
    cut in half

Dressing:

**Good Seasons® Italian packet (Substitute with
balsamic vinegar and olive oil)**

Prepare dressing and set aside.

Place salad ingredients in large bowl. Refrigerate to chill. Just before serving, gently toss all ingredients with desired amount of dressing.

Note: Artichokes may be cut into bite-sized pieces. Cooked shrimp may also be cut into bite-sized pieces, if necessary. Orange bell pepper may be added for more color. Add more mushrooms and tomatoes, if desired.

Note: Terry Arakaki, who taught with me at Kainalu Elementary many years ago shared this great potluck salad recipe that she had gotten from her friend, Cindy Dela-Cruz.

Chicken Cucumber Salad

yield: 6–8 servings

* *

3 to 4 boneless skinless chicken breasts,
   cooked and shredded
4 to 5 cucumbers, cut into 2-inch lengths, then into strips
2 stalks green onions, thinly sliced

Sauce:

1/2 cup sugar
1/2 cup Japanese vinegar
1/4 cup sesame oil
2 teaspoons hondashi
1/2 cup soy sauce
3 tablespoons sesame seeds
2 cloves garlic, minced

Combine sauce ingredients; refrigerate. Refrigerate chicken, cucumbers and green onions. When ready to serve, mix everything together.

Chicken or Turkey Salad

yield: 4–6 servings

* *

2 cups cooked cold chicken (thighs or breasts) or turkey,
   cut into cubes
2 stalks celery, chopped (about 1 cup)
2 hardboiled eggs, chopped
1 tablespoon lemon juice
1/2 cup mayonnaise (begin with less and adjust to taste)
Salt and pepper to taste
Tomato wedges or slices for garnish (optional)

Mix all ingredients together; chill. Serve on lettuce; garnish with tomatoes, if desired.

Chinese Chicken Salad

yield: 10–12 servings

* *

1 head iceberg lettuce, torn into bite-sized pieces
3 stalks celery, thinly sliced
1/4 cup green onion, chopped
2 to 3 romaine lettuce leaves, cut into bite-sized pieces (optional)
1 bunch Chinese parsley, chopped (optional)
1 package boiled ham, 8 slices (6 oz.), cut into thin strips
2 to 3 chicken breasts, cooked in lightly salted water, shredded
20 sheets wun tun pi, cut into thin strips and deep-fried,
   or 1 can La Choy® Chow Mein Noodles

Dressing:

4 tablespoons sugar
2 teaspoons salt
1 teaspoon pepper
1/2 cup Wesson® oil
6 tablespoons vinegar
1/2 teaspoon sesame oil

Combine dressing ingredients. Place in jar and shake well.

Mix all vegetables and refrigerate. Just before serving, add ham and chicken and toss. Pour desired amount of dressing over and toss. Add desired amount of wun tun pi or noodles; toss lightly.

Note: There are many wonderful Chinese Chicken Salad recipes, but this is our favorite. It is simple with a light refreshing dressing. It tastes great at any potluck gathering.

Chinese Chicken Salad with Peanut Dressing

yield: 8–10 servings as a side dish

* *

1-1/2 pounds chicken breast
2 cups water
1 stalk green onion, chopped
1 slice fresh ginger, about 1 inch
1 tablespoon sherry
1/2 teaspoon salt
1/2 teaspoon sugar
1 large head iceberg lettuce, shredded
Chinese parsley for garnish, if desired

Bring water, green onion, ginger, sherry, salt and sugar to boil; add chicken. Lower heat and simmer about 20 minutes. Remove chicken; cool and shred. Put lettuce into salad bowl and top with chicken; chill. Toss with Peanut Dressing just before serving and garnish with Chinese parsley, if desired.

Peanut Dressing:

1-1/2 tablespoons creamy peanut butter
2-1/2 tablespoons oil
2 tablespoons sugar
2 tablespoons soy sauce
2 teaspoons vinegar
1-1/2 teaspoons sesame oil
1/4 to 1/2 teaspoon ground chili pepper or cayenne pepper
1 tablespoon round onion, grated

Combine all ingredients in bowl and mix well.

Note: Very tasty. The amount of dressing is just enough for a lightly seasoned salad. You may want to double the dressing recipe.

Hot and Spicy Chinese Chicken Salad

yield: 12–15 serving as a side dish

✳ ✳

3 chicken breasts or 4 thighs, boneless and skinless
1 cup cashews, coarsely chopped
1 or 2 bundles long rice threads (2 oz. each), cut into 2-inch
    lengths (see "Note" below)
1 small head iceberg lettuce, thinly sliced and chilled
Oil for deep-frying
Toasted sesame seeds for sprinkling
Chinese parsley for garnish

Dressing:

3 tablespoons dry mustard
4 tablespoons oyster sauce
4 tablespoons sesame oil
4 teaspoons sugar
1 teaspoon chili oil (adjust to taste)

Combine dressing ingredients and mix; set aside.

Dredging mixture for chicken:

1/4 cup flour
1 tablespoon fine Panko® or cornmeal
1/2 teaspoon Chinese five spice
1/2 teaspoon salt

Combine dredging ingredients and mix. Coat chicken in
dredging mixture; set aside.

(continued on next page)

Heat about 1-1/2 inches of oil and deep-fry noodles until puffy; drain and set aside. Using same oil, fry chicken until cooked and crisp; drain. Cool and slice into 1/4-inch strips.

Coat chicken and cashews with dressing. When ready to serve, toss lettuce and noodles; add chicken and cashews and toss lightly. Sprinkle with sesame seeds and garnish with parsley.

Note: The long rice threads are very difficult to cut. Straighten the folded rice threads and separate the threads into smaller groups. Then cut with kitchen shears a little at a time. One bundle of rice threads puffs up to a lot so be prepared with a large container to store the puffed rice noodles until ready to use. One bundle is sufficient for a small head of lettuce, but you may prefer having more long rice as the puffed long rice quickly wilts in the salad.

Easy Caesar Salad
yield: 6 servings as a side dish

* *

1 head romaine lettuce, torn into bite-sized pieces
1 cup croutons
1/2 cup Caesar salad dressing (e.g., use Kraft® Free Caesar
Italian Dressing or your favorite brand)
3 tablespoons parmesan cheese, grated (adjust to taste)

Place lettuce in large salad bowl. Add croutons and dressing; toss lightly. Sprinkle with parmesan cheese.

Note: This is a quick and tasty salad to prepare when you are busy. Just be sure that the romaine lettuce is chilled and crisp.

Easy French Dressing

yield: 2 cups

* *

1 cup oil
3/4 cup sugar
1/3 cup vinegar
3/4 cup catsup
Pepper to taste (optional)
1 clove garlic, minced (optional)

Combine ingredients and blend well with whisk. Refrigerate.

Ritz Salad Dressing

yield: 2 cups

* *

1 cup sugar
1 cup oil
1 cup catsup
1/4 cup vinegar
1 tablespoon salt
1 tablespoon lemon juice
1 tablespoon onion, minced (optional)

Combine ingredients and blend well with whisk. Refrigerate.

Note: These are two favorite salad dressings recommended by Sharyn Masukawa, my mother's friend in Hilo. She hopes that others will enjoy them, too.

Club Dressing

yield: about 2 cups

* *

Group A:

1 cup oil
3/4 cup sugar
1/2 cup white vinegar (or Japanese vinegar)
1/3 cup Best Foods® mayonnaise
2-1/2 teaspoons salt
1/4 teaspoon pepper
1/4 teaspoon Worcestershire sauce
1/2 teaspoon prepared mustard
2 tablespoons sesame oil
1/2 small onion, cut in pieces
1 clove garlic, cut in pieces

Group B:

1 tablespoon toasted sesame seeds
Juice from 1/2 lemon

Blend Group A ingredients about 1 minute. Add Group B and blend a little longer.

Note: This popular dressing recipe has been passed around and shared for many years and it's still great. Thanks, Mimi and Steve, for sharing it with me.

Jake's Diabetic
Chinese Salad Dressing
yield: 2-1/2 cups

* *

3/4 cup lemon juice (about 3 to 4 ripe lemons)
3/4 cup Japanese vinegar
1 cup Wesson® oil
4 teaspoons salt
2 teaspoons pepper
12 packages Equal® or Splenda®

Whisk dressing ingredients to blend. Refrigerate.

Note: When Jake Shiraki was eight years old, he learned about diabetes from his nana, Evelyn Shiraki, who is a nurse. He found this recipe and shared it with her diabetic patients. It is tasty. (Jake was a kindergarten student of mine at Aikahi Elementary School and I am proud of him. He now lives with his family in Kamuela on the Big Island.)

Miso Dressing
yield: about 2 cups

* *

1 cup miso
1/4 cup rice vinegar
1/4 cup sake
1/4 cup soy sauce
1 cup sugar
1 teaspoon lemon juice
3 teaspoons fresh ginger juice
1 teaspoon sesame seed, ground in suribachi

Blend miso with vinegar, sake and soy sauce before adding rest of the ingredients. Mix together and use over green vegetables.

Note: A suribachi is a Japanese serrated bowl which is used to crush the sesame seeds using a wooden pestle. Small suribachi bowls are sold at some supermarkets. I also use it to pulverize Hawaiian salt to make "Mimi's Shrimp" found in *Hawai'i's Best Pūpū & Potluck* cookbook.

Tropics Dressing

yield: approximately 3-1/2 cups

* *

1/2 cup sugar
1/3 cup mayonnaise
1-1/2 cups oil
1 cup catsup
3 tablespoons apple cider
1 tablespoon prepared mustard
2-1/3 teaspoons salt
1 tablespoon Worchestershire sauce
4 teaspoons lemon juice
1 teaspoon soy sauce
1 teaspoon fresh garlic, minced

Combine all in a bowl and mix with beater until smooth.

Note: Highly recommended by Evelyn Shiraki. A fresh great-tasting dressing for your green salads!

Crab Salad

yield: 15 servings as a side dish

* *

1 package spaghetti (16-oz.)
1 can crab (6-oz.), drained
12-oz. imitation crab, shredded
Juice of one lemon
1 cucumber
Mayonnaise to moisten
Salt
Pepper

Break spaghetti in thirds and cook according to package directions. Rinse and drain well; let sit at least 30 minutes. Score on skin of cucumber. Cut cucumber in half lengthwise and seed; slice thinly. Sprinkle with salt; let stand about 20 minutes. Drain well; squeeze out excess water. Combine spaghetti, crab, lemon juice and enough mayonnaise to moisten. Salt and pepper to taste. Chill before serving.

Note: Prepare a day ahead because it tastes better the next day.

German Potato Salad

yield: 4–6 servings as a side dish

✳ ✳

3 medium potatoes, boiled in skins
3 slices bacon
1/4 cup onion, chopped
1 tablespoon flour
2 teaspoons sugar
3/4 teaspoon salt
1/4 teaspoon celery seeds
1/4 teaspoon pepper
3/8 cup water
2-1/2 tablespoons vinegar

Peel cooked potatoes and slice thin. Fry bacon slowly in large pan; drain on paper towels. Crumble bacon and set aside. Sauté onion in bacon fat until golden brown. Combine flour, sugar, salt, celery seeds and pepper and blend with sautéed onions. Cook over low heat, stirring until smooth and bubbly. Remove from heat. Stir in water and vinegar. Return to heat and bring to boil, stirring constantly. Boil for 1 minute. Carefully stir in potatoes and crumbled bacon. Remove from heat; cover and let stand until ready to serve.

Pasta Salad (Page 51)

Strawberry Salad
(Page 91)

Broccoli Shrimp Salad (Page 56)

Sesame Asparagus
(Page 129)

Bean Salad (Page 52)

Chinese Chicken Salad (Page 58)

Okinawan Sweet Potato Salad (Page 76)

Minestrone Soup (Page 23)

Seafood Bisque (Page 37)

Ga Hap Ca (Steamed Chicken with Tomatoes) (Page 14)

Mushroom Soup (Page 3)

Jello O Fruit Salad (Page 70)

Hot Potato Salad

yield: 8–10 servings as a side dish

* *

3/4 cup fresh shrimp (51 to 60 count size), boiled,
    shelled and cut into thirds
1 can crabmeat (6 oz.), shredded
4 medium potatoes, boiled and cubed
1/4 cup onion, minced
1/4 cup celery, chopped
1 cup mayonnaise
1/2 teaspoon Worcestershire sauce
1/4 teaspoon pepper
1/2 teaspoon salt

Topping:

1/2 cup bread crumbs
2 tablespoons butter, melted

Mix salad ingredients together. Place in 9 × 9-inch dish. Top with bread crumbs and melted butter. Bake at 350°F for 20 minutes.

Jell-O® Fruit Salad

yield: 24 pieces

* *

1 can pear halves, lite (15 oz.), drained; reserve liquid
2 cans sliced peaches, lite (15 oz. each), drained; reserve liquid
1 can fruit cocktail, lite (15 oz.), drained; reserve liquid
2 large boxes strawberry Jell-O® (6 oz. each)
6-1/2 cups liquid (combine juice from fruit and hot water)
2 packages Knox® gelatin
1/2 cup water
1 box cream cheese (8 oz.), softened at room temperature
2 to 3 tablespoons mayonnaise

Drain fruits; reserve liquid. Cut pear halves in thirds lengthwise. Place drained fruits in bowl; set aside.

Add enough hot water to fruit liquid to make 6-1/2 cups liquid; mix together with Strawberry JellO®. Combine Knox® gelatin and 1/2 cup water and mix into Jell-O® mixture. Pour into 9 × 13-inch pan. Refrigerate until slightly set (about 1 hour).

Blend together cream cheese and mayonnaise; fold into fruits. Then fold fruit and cream mixture into partially jelled Jell-O®. Refrigerate until firm.

Note: Very refreshing! The cream cheese mixture added to the fruits gives this Jell-O® fruit salad a little something extra beyond the ordinary Jell-O® and fruit combination. Try substituting lime or orange Jell-O®.

Kim Chee Salad

yield: 10–12 servings as a side dish

* *

1 small head cabbage, sliced
2 tablespoons Hawaiian salt
1 small carrot, julienned
4 stalks green onions, thinly sliced

Seasoning:

5 cloves garlic, minced
2 teaspoons toasted sesame oil
1 teaspoon Noh® kim chee powder, or 1-1/2 teaspoons
    crushed red pepper; adjust to taste
3 teaspoons sugar
2 teaspoons sesame oil
1 tablespoon vegetable oil
1/2 cup vinegar

Sprinkle salt over cabbage; toss. Set aside 20 minutes. Prepare seasoning; set aside.

Squeeze cabbage and place in large bowl. Pour seasoning over and toss well. Refrigerate, tossing at intervals. Let sit for better flavor before serving.

Long Rice Salad
yield: 8–10 servings

* *

3 packages long rice (1-7/8 oz. each)
Salt to taste
1 egg, beaten, fried in thin sheet and thinly sliced
1 cucumber, seeded and thinly sliced
1/4 cup green onions, thinly sliced
1/4 pound ham, thinly sliced
1 cup cabbage, shredded
1/2 pound imitation crab, shredded

Dressing:

1/3 cup sugar
1/3 cup vinegar
2 tablespoons soy sauce
1 teaspoon ginger juice
2 teaspoons sesame oil

Combine dressing ingredients and set aside.

Cook long rice in lightly salted boiling water until tender, about 10 to 15 minutes. Drain and rinse in cold water; cut into 3-inch lengths. Mix egg, cucumber, green onion and ham with long rice. Stir in cabbage and crab. Combine dressing ingredients and pour over mixture, tossing gently. Chill.

Note: Gladys Fuchigami brought this popular potluck to a family gathering. It's refreshing and a great side dish to complement the many other dishes. She said she likes to use a combination of white vinegar and Japanese vinegar to equal the 1/3 cup vinegar.

Long Rice Salad with Fish Sauce

yield: 4 servings

* *

2 boneless and skinless chicken thighs, boiled and shredded
1 bundle long rice (2 oz.)
1/4 round onion, thinly sliced
1 tray fresh mushrooms (8 oz.), sliced
1 clove garlic, chopped
2 eggs, beaten, fried and chopped
1/4 cup green onions, thinly sliced
Chinese parsley to garnish (optional)

Sauce:

1-1/2 tablespoons fish sauce
1-1/2 teaspoons lime juice
1/2 teaspoon chili sauce

Mix sauce ingredients and set aside. Add long rice to boiling water and cook until transparent (about 5 minutes). Rinse in cold water and drain well. Cut long rice roughly into 2-inch lengths. Sauté mushrooms and garlic for a few minutes until limp.

Layer salad in the following order: long rice, onions, mushrooms, eggs, green onions and chicken. Garnish with Chinese parsley, if desired. Refrigerate. Pour sauce over salad just before serving.

Mandarin Orange Gelatin

yield: 24 servings

* *

1 can sliced peaches (15 oz.), drained (reserve 3 tablespoons
   peach syrup)
4 packages unflavored gelatin (e.g., Knox® gelatin)
1 cup boiling water
1 package cream cheese (8 oz.), softened at room temperature
1 cup sugar
1 cup 7-up®
1/2 teaspoon lemon juice
1 teaspoon almond extract
2 cans mandarin oranges (11 oz.), drained (large
   Del Monte® brand)
1 jar maraschino cherries (6 oz.), cut in half (optional)

In small bowl add 3 tablespoons peach syrup to unflavored gelatin; mix together. Add boiling water, beginning with small amount of hot water and blend until smooth. Add rest; mix and set aside to cool.

In large bowl, beat cream cheese and sugar. Add gelatin mixture and blend together. Add 7-up®, lemon juice, almond extract, peaches and oranges; mix. Pour into 9 × 13-inch pan greased with mayonnaise. Refrigerate to set. Cut into 24 pieces and garnish with 1/2 cherries, if desired.

Note: Very refreshing and light. Thanks to my neighbor, Evelyn Shiraki, who improved the original recipe and shared it with me.

Ocean Somen Salad

yield: 6–8 servings

* *

1 package somen (8 oz.), cooked as directed on package,
    drained and cooled
2 eggs, beaten
1 kamaboko (6 oz.), thinly sliced into strips
1 small round sweet onion thinly sliced
1/4 pound ocean salad
1/2 cup char siu, thinly sliced
1 stalk green onion, chopped

Dressing:

1 teaspoon salt
2 tablespoons roasted sesame seeds
2 tablespoons sugar
2 tablespoons soy sauce
3 tablespoons (Japanese) rice vinegar
4 tablespoons canola oil

Fry beaten eggs into a sheet and slice into thin strips. Mix together somen and ocean salad. Add kamaboko, onion and eggs; mix lightly. Garnish with green onions and char siu. Refrigerate. Combine dressing ingredients in jar; shake well. When ready to serve, shake dressing well and pour over salad.

Okinawan Sweet Potato Salad

yield: 8 servings as a side dish

* *

3 small Okinawan potatoes (purple flesh)
1 small sweet potato (white flesh)
1 large yellow yam
2 to 3 cloves garlic, minced or 1 tablespoon
    chopped onion (adjust to taste)
Juice of 1/4 lemon
1 stalk celery, chopped
1/2 cup green peas, blanched (optional)
Mayonnaise, to moisten

Peel and cut potatoes into cubes. Cook each type of potato separately in lightly salted boiling water until done (about 7 minutes each). When done, drain and set aside to cool. Combine cooled potatoes with rest of ingredients and refrigerate to chill.

Note: The purple, white and yellow potatoes make this a colorful and flavorful salad. Sayoko Watanabe introduced me to this unique salad. I made it for a luncheon and it was a big hit.

Pine Nut Salad

* *

1 head romaine lettuce, cut into bite-sized pieces
1/2 cup green onions, chopped
1/4 cup pine nuts, roasted at 350°F for 5 minutes
6 fresh mushrooms, sliced
1 can sliced olives (2.25 oz.), drained
Croutons (optional)

Dressing:

1/2 cup olive oil
1/4 teaspoon salt
2 teaspoons white wine vinegar
1 teaspoon Dijon mustard
1/4 cup parmesan cheese
2 cloves garlic, crushed

Combine dressing ingredients; shake well. Just before serving pour dressing over salad and toss lightly.

Variation: Substitute slivered almonds for pine nuts (not necessary to roast almonds).

Note: This salad with the great tasting dressing was first shared by Sharon Smith at an Aikahi Elementary potluck many years ago. Since then it's been a favorite of mine. Everyone asks for this recipe as soon as they taste it.

Pineapple Molded Salad

yield: 15–20 servings as a side dish

* *

1 can crushed pineapple (20 oz.), *do not drain*
1/2 cup sugar
Juice of 1/2 lemon
2 packages Knox® gelatin dissolved in 1/2 cup water
1 cup small curd cottage cheese
1/2 cup finely shredded mild cheddar cheese
1 cup whipping cream, *do not whip*

Combine crushed pineapple and sugar in saucepan. Heat until sugar is dissolved. Turn heat off. Add lemon juice and dissolved gelatin; mix together and place in refrigerator. When mixture begins to set (about 1 hour), add rest of ingredients and pour into 1-quart ring mold greased with mayonnaise. Refrigerate to set.

Note: When ready to unmold, briefly run hot water over overturned ring mold. Place upside down on platter and pineapple molded salad will drop down. If mold is unavailable, use 8 × 8-inch pan.

Poke Salad

yield: 9 × 13-inch pan

* *

1 medium Chinese cabbage (won bok), thinly shredded
1 cup cabbage, thinly shredded
1/2 to 1 pound poke (e.g., ahi limu poke), cut into small pieces
1/2 cup chopped walnuts
1/4 cup raisins

Suggested dressings:

Gyotaku® Sweet and Sour Dressing
Tropics® Original Oriental Sesame Seed Dressing

In 9 × 13-inch pan, layer ingredients in order listed. Refrigerate until ready to serve. Have individuals serve themselves and use dressing of choice.

Note: At a social gathering on Maui, Glenn Oura presented this potluck dish, a very unusual combination with poke, walnuts and raisins. Glenn said he had tasted a similar salad at an upscale restaurant and liked it so he came up with his own poke salad. He didn't tell me what dressing he used but I experimented and found several I liked. Listed above are two. My neighbor said she likes using the common mustard and soy sauce as the dressing.

Red Cabbage Coleslaw

yield: 10–12 servings as a side dish

* *

1/2 medium head cabbage, shredded
1 small head red cabbage, shredded
3/4 cup sugar (divided)
1/2 medium onion
1-1/2 teaspoons salt
1 teaspoon prepared mustard
1 cup vinegar
3/4 cup oil

In large bowl, toss cabbage with 3/4 cup less 1 teaspoon sugar. Set aside.

Slice half onion thinly and separate half circles.

In another large bowl, layer cabbage and onion rings. Mix 1 teaspoon sugar, salt, mustard and vinegar in saucepan and bring to boil. Add oil to mixture and remove from heat. While hot, pour mixture over cabbage; do not stir. Cover and refrigerate for 24 to 48 hours. Stir and drain before serving.

Soba Salad

yield: 10–12 servings

* *

1 package buckwheat noodles (yamaimo soba 8.75 oz.),
   e.g., Ishiguro® brand
1/2 pound ocean salad
1/2 Maui onion or sweet onion, thinly sliced
1/2 pound imitation crab, shredded
1 package baby spinach leaves (6 oz.) or 1 bunch spinach
1 tomato, thinly sliced

Break soba noodles in half before cooking. Cook soba as directed on package. Drain well. Place soba on large platter or in 9 × 13-inch pan. Top with ocean salad, sliced onions, imitation crab, spinach and tomatoes in that order.

Dressing:

1/2 cup sugar
1/2 to 1 teaspoon black pepper
2 teaspoons salt
1/3 cup Japanese vinegar
1/2 cup or less vegetable oil
1 tablespoon sesame oil
2 to 3 teaspoons lemon juice (about 1/2 lemon)

Mix well until sugar is dissolved. Pour over salad before serving.

Variation: Substitute spinach with chopped watercress.

Note: On one of my trips to Hilo, my cousin, Miye Watanabe, introduced me to this very popular soba salad doing the rounds in Hilo. It's a great potluck salad. The dressing is especially delicious!

Somen Salad

yield: 9 × 13-inch pan

* *

1 package somen (8 oz.), noodles broken in half and
  cooked according to package directions
1 small head iceberg lettuce, shredded
1 bunch Chinese parsley, chopped (optional)
3 stalks green onion, finely chopped
1 cucumber, julienned
1 kamaboko (6-oz.), thinly sliced and cut into thin strips
3 eggs, beaten and fried, thinly sliced into 2-inch strips
1/4 pound char siu or ham, thinly sliced

Dressing:

1 tablespoon roasted sesame seeds
2 tablespoons sugar
1 teaspoon salt
3 tablespoons vinegar
2 tablespoons soy sauce
1/4 cup oil

Layer salad ingredients in order listed in 9 × 13-inch pan.
Refrigerate. Combine dressing ingredients and shake well.
Serve salad in individual portions and pour desired amount
of dressing over.

Note: I usually double the dressing so that there's more than
enough for generous helpings.

Shabu Shabu Beef Salad

yield: 12–15 servings

* *

1 pound boneless teriyaki or sukiyaki meat, thinly sliced,
  cut into 1/2-inch strips
1 small head iceberg lettuce, shredded
1 package bean sprouts (10 oz.)
1 package radish sprouts (4 oz.), cut off roots,
  wash sprouts and drain

Sauce:

1/2 cup daikon, grated
1 cup ponzu

Boil water and cook bean sprouts (about 1 minute). Rinse with water; drain.

Boil water and cook thinly sliced beef until color is changed (about 1 minute). Rinse with water; drain. Set aside.

Mix lettuce and bean sprouts and place mixture on platter. Place beef over lettuce. Top with radish sprouts over all. Serve with sauce.

Seaweed–Soba Salad

yield: 10–12 servings

* *

1/2 cup hijiki or kurome, soaked in warm water 20 minutes
3 tablespoons olive oil
3 tablespoons soy sauce
3 tablespoons sugar

Drain hijiki and squeeze out water. In skillet, heat olive oil. Add hijiki and stir-fry. Add soy sauce and sugar and cook until all liquid is absorbed. Set aside to cool.

1 package wakame (0.25 oz.), soaked in water 15 minutes
2 packages buckwheat soba (8 oz. each)
1/2 Maui onion, thinly sliced
1 container daikon sprouts (4 oz.), ends trimmed
1 bunch watercress, cut into 1-inch pieces

Drain wakame and squeeze out liquid. Cut into bite-sized pieces; set aside. Cook soba in boiling water 5 to 7 minutes; rinse and drain well.

Layer salad ingredients on large platter in this order: soba, hijiki, onion, daikon sprouts, watercress, and wakame.

Dressing:

3/4 cup olive oil
3/4 cup soy sauce
1/4 cup sugar
1/4 cup + 2 tablespoons lemon juice

Combine dressing ingredients and pour over salad 15 minutes before serving.

Optional: Garnish with julienned kamaboko or imitation crabmeat.

Warabi Tofu Salad

yield: 8–10 servings as a side dish

* *

1 bunch warabi (about 40 stalks)
10 to 12 dried shrimp, cut in half
1/2 cup round onion, thinly sliced
1 block firm tofu (20 oz.), cut into 1-inch cubes

Dressing:

2 tablespoons brown sugar
8 tablespoons soy sauce
4 tablespoons lemon juice
6 tablespoons vegetable oil

Combine dressing ingredients. Mix well and set aside.

Clean warabi and cut into 1-1/2-inch slices. Place into boiling water for about 30 seconds. Drain; place into iced water for 15 minutes. Drain again. Place warabi in bowl. Add shrimp, onion and tofu. Pour dressing over and gently toss together. Refrigerate before serving.

Spaghetti Salad

yield: 15–20 servings as a side dish

* *

1 package spaghetti (16 oz.)
1 cucumber, thinly sliced
3 stalks celery, sliced
2 tomatoes, cubed
1/2 green bell pepper, thinly sliced
1/2 Maui onion, thinly sliced
6 red globe radishes, sliced

Seasoning:

1 cup Italian dressing (8 oz.)
1 bottle chili sauce (12 oz.)
Garlic salt to taste (optional)
Onion salt to taste (optional)
Seasoned salt to taste (optional)
Seasoned pepper to taste (optional)
Celery seeds to taste (optional)
Romano cheese, grated, for garnish (optional)

Break spaghetti in half and cook spaghetti following package directions; rinse in cold water and drain. Let sit 15 to 20 minutes to "air dry." Place spaghetti in large bowl and add vegetables.

Toss salad with Italian dressing, chili sauce and any or all of the other seasonings to your taste. Garnish with grated romano cheese, if desired. Chill before serving.

Note: Instead of pouring the entire 12-oz. bottle of chili sauce over salad, you may want to begin with 3/4 of the bottle and add more, as needed. May be prepared a day ahead. Tastes even better the next day.

Note: Amy Shimizu Oshiro, an old friend from Hilo High days, was so sweet to share this great potluck salad with us.

Spinach Salad

* *

1 bunch spinach, torn into bite-sized pieces
1 cup bean sprouts
1 can water chestnuts (5 oz.), sliced
2 eggs, hard-boiled and finely chopped
6 slices bacon, fried and finely chopped

Dressing:

1 cup salad oil
1/4 teaspoon salt
2 tablespoons sugar
2 teaspoons Worcestershire sauce
1/4 cup vinegar
1/2 cup catsup
1/4 cup onion, finely grated

Combine dressing ingredients; shake well. Refrigerate to chill.

Layer salad ingredients in large bowl in the order listed. Pour desired amount of dressing over just before serving.

Note: I really like this particular dressing for this salad. You may add more grated onion to the dressing, if you prefer a sharper taste.

Spinach Salad with Almonds

yield: 4–6 servings

* *

1 bunch spinach (about 6 cups), washed and stems removed
1/2 cup red bell pepper, julienned
1/4 cup slivered almonds

Dressing:

1/4 cup sugar
1/3 cup red wine vinegar
1/3 cup vegetable oil
2 tablespoons shallots, diced
2 tablespoons garlic, diced
1/2 teaspoon salt
1 teaspoon dry mustard

Combine dressing ingredients; shake well and set aside. Combine spinach and red pepper and refrigerate to chill. Just before serving, add almonds. Shake salad dressing and pour desired amount over. Toss gently.

Spinach–Tomato–Bacon Salad

yield: 4 servings

✳ ✳

3 large bunches spinach, washed and cleaned, or
    2 bags washed spinach (7.75 oz. each)
2 tomatoes, cut into bite-sized chunks
10 slices bacon, chopped
1 small Maui onion, julienned
1 tablespoon garlic, finely chopped
1/2 cup white balsamic vinegar
1 teaspoon fresh lemon juice
1/4 cup extra virgin olive oil
1 tablespoon Dijon mustard
1/2 teaspoon sugar
2 teaspoons garlic salt
6 large basil leaves, julienned
Salt and pepper to taste
Feta cheese, crumbled, for garnish
1 hard-boiled Egg, finely chopped, for garnish

Place spinach and tomatoes in large salad bowl. Set aside.

Sauté bacon until crispy; remove from pan and set aside. In same pan with bacon drippings, sauté onion and garlic until slightly tender. Add vinegar and lemon juice. Stir, dislodging browned bacon bits from pan. Remove pan from heat; add oil, mustard, sugar, garlic salt and basil. Use whisk to mix well. Season with salt and pepper.

Pour desired amount of warm dressing over spinach and tomatoes and toss together. Sprinkle with bacon. Garnish with feta cheese and egg.

Spinach Salad with Hot Dressing

yield: 4 servings

* *

1 bunch spinach, stems removed
1 cup fresh mushrooms (about 4 to 5 mushrooms), sliced
4 stalks green onions, thinly sliced
1 to 2 hard-boiled eggs, diced (for garnish)

Combine spinach, mushrooms and green onions. Set aside diced eggs for garnish.

Dressing:

6 slices bacon
1/4 cup vinegar
2 tablespoons water
1/2 teaspoon salt
1/4 teaspoon pepper (or less)
1/4 teaspoon dry mustard

Fry bacon until brown; drain and dice. Set aside. Drain bacon fat from frying pan; add vinegar, water, salt, pepper and mustard. Blend well. Bring to a boil for 1 to 2 minutes. Mix in diced bacon.

Pour hot dressing over salad and toss lightly. Sprinkle diced egg over salad. Serve immediately.

Variation: Substitute 1/4 cup round onion, thinly slivered, for green onions. Add sliced olives as garnish.

Strawberry Salad

yield: 4–6 servings

* *

1 bunch spinach, torn into bite-sized pieces
2 cups fresh strawberries, chopped
1/2 cup pecans, chopped
2 tablespoons butter

Dressing:

1/4 cup red onion, thinly sliced
1 cup oil
1/3 cup red wine vinegar
1/2 teaspoon salt
1/2 cup sugar
1 teaspoon dry mustard
1 teaspoon poppy seeds

Mix dressing ingredients and set aside. Melt butter and mix in chopped pecans. Toast buttered pecans in 350°F oven for 10 minutes. Toss together with spinach and strawberries. Pour dressing over spinach mixture.

Note: A surprisingly tasty combination, this salad has caught on in recent years. It is quite popular now.

Sweet Potato Salad

yield: 6 servings as a side dish

* *

2 pounds sweet potatoes, scrubbed, quartered lengthwise
  and cut crosswise into 3/4-inch pieces
2 tablespoons green onions, thinly sliced
1/4 cup sweet red pepper, finely chopped (optional)

Dressing:

3 tablespoons cider vinegar
2 tablespoons sweet pickle relish
2 teaspoons Dijon mustard
1/2 teaspoon salt
1/4 teaspoon pepper
1/2 cup oil

Combine vinegar, pickle relish, mustard, salt and pepper in a
jar with a tight-fitting lid. Mix well. Add oil and shake well.
Set aside.

Steam or boil sweet potatoes for 10 to 15 minutes or until
tender. Drain and cool potatoes 10 minutes. Peel and place
potatoes in serving bowl. Shake dressing well and pour over
warm potatoes. Toss potatoes. Add green onions and red
pepper, if desired. Serve at room temperature or chilled.

Taco Salad

yield: 12 servings

* *

1 head iceberg lettuce
1 green bell pepper, sliced
1 medium package corn chips (10 oz.)
1/2 onion, minced
2 firm ripe tomatoes, cubed
10 pitted black olives, sliced
1 pound ground beef
1 package taco seasoning mix (1.25 oz.)
3/4 cup water

Wash and break lettuce into bite-sized pieces. In large salad bowl, put lettuce, green pepper, corn chips, onion, tomatoes, and olives; chill.

Brown ground beef; drain. Add taco seasoning and water; mix well and bring to boil. Reduce heat and simmer 15 minutes. Just before serving, pour taco mixture over vegetables.

Taegu Ocean Salad Linguine

yield: 10–12 servings

* *

1 package linguine (8 oz.), break into thirds and cook
   according to package directions, drain and cool
3 ounces taegu
2 Japanese cucumbers, seeded and sliced into 1-inch strips
8 ounces imitation crab, shredded
8 ounces fresh green ocean salad
1/2 bottle furikake (half of 1.9 oz.), adjust to taste
Tropics® Oriental Dressing (12 oz.), adjust to taste
Chinese parsley (for garnish), optional

Mix cooked linguine with taegu, cucumbers, imitation crab
and ocean salad. Just before serving, mix in desired amount
of Tropics® Oriental Dressing to taste. Garnish with Chinese
parsley, if desired.

Note: This recipe originated from Linda Shimamoto via
Ruby Saito to me. This is a very popular potluck dish with
locals.

Thai Noodle Salad
with Peanut Sauce

yield: 8 servings as a side dish

* *

1 box angel hair pasta (12 oz.)
3 tablespoons sesame oil
1/2 cup green onions, thinly sliced
2 tablespoons Chinese parsley, chopped
2 to 3 cups bean sprouts, blanched
1 cup carrots, shredded or julienned
1 cup dry roasted unsalted peanuts, chopped

Sauce:

1 cup soy sauce
1 cup creamy peanut butter
1 cup honey
1-1/2 tablespoons chili–garlic sauce
3 tablespoons rice vinegar
1 tablespoon vegetable oil
1 inch fresh ginger, chopped
5 garlic cloves, chopped

Whisk together soy sauce, peanut butter, honey, chili–garlic sauce and rice vinegar; set aside. In sauté pan, heat vegetable oil to medium high heat. Stir in ginger and garlic. Add peanut butter mixture; whisk to blend in and simmer for 1 minute. Cool to room temperature and set aside. Yield: about 3 cups.

Cook pasta in large amount of boiling salted water. When tender, but still firm, drain and toss with sesame oil. Pour 1/2 cup sauce over pasta and toss in green onions, Chinese parsley, bean sprouts, carrots and peanuts. Add more sauce to taste, as desired. Refrigerate remaining sauce in refrigerator for later use.

Tofu Salad

yield: 10 servings

* *

1 block firm tofu (20 oz.), cubed
1/2 Maui onion, thinly sliced
1 can salmon (7.5 oz.) or 1 can tuna (6 oz.)
1 package bean sprouts (10 oz.), parboiled,
    drained and cooled (optional)
1 bunch watercress, cut into 1-1/2-inch pieces
1 to 2 tomatoes, cubed

Layer all the above in order listed in large salad bowl or platter, starting with tofu on the bottom. Place in refrigerator until ready to serve.

Dressing:

1/4 cup vegetable oil
1 tablespoon sesame oil
1 clove garlic
1/2 cup soy sauce

Heat vegetable oil, sesame oil and garlic until garlic is browned. Remove from heat and cool. Add soy sauce to cooled oil. Pour over salad just before serving.

Note: My nephew, Henry Watanabe, often requests Grandma Watanabe to prepare this salad for him. To me, this dressing is the best of all the tofu salad dressings out there.

Tuna Macaroni Salad

yield: 8–10 servings

* *

2 cups uncooked macaroni
4 medium potatoes
1 package frozen peas (10 oz.)
5 to 6 hard-boiled eggs, cut into bite-sized pieces
1/4 onion, finely diced
1/4 cup celery, finely diced
2 tablespoons sweet pickle relish
1 can tuna (6 oz.), drained
1 cup mayonnaise, adjust to just moisten ingredients
Salt and pepper to taste

Boil macaroni in salted water until tender; drain and cool. Peel potatoes; cut into bite-sized pieces and boil in salted water until tender. Drain and cool. Defrost peas in 1/2-inch of salted hot water; drain. In small bowl, combine diced onion, celery and sweet pickle relish; set aside. In large bowl, mix all ingredients to create desired consistency. Season with salt and pepper. Refrigerate, covered, until serving time.

24-Hour Lettuce Salad

yield: 8–10 servings as a side dish

* *

1 head iceberg lettuce, sliced
1 cucumber, sliced
1/4 cup celery, thinly sliced
1 can water chestnuts (8 oz.), sliced
1 package frozen peas (10 oz.), *do not thaw*
2 cups mayonnaise

Place lettuce in salad bowl. Add cucumbers, celery, water chestnuts and frozen peas in that order. Spread mayonnaise over vegetables like frosting.

1/2 cup parmesan cheese, grated
2 teaspoons sugar
1 teaspoon salt (or seasoned salt)
1/4 teaspoon garlic salt
Bacon bits for garnish
2 tomatoes, sliced
6 hard-boiled eggs, sliced

Mix together parmesan cheese, sugar, salt and garlic salt and sprinkle over mayonnaise. Cover and refrigerate overnight. Before serving, garnish with bacon bits, sliced tomatoes and eggs.

24-Hour Salad with Shrimp

yield: Serves 8–10 as a side dish

* *

1 head iceberg lettuce, sliced
1/4 cup onion, chopped
1 bunch Chinese parsley, chopped (about 1 cup)
1 cucumber, julienned (seeded if necessary)
1 package frozen peas (10 oz.), *do not thaw*
1/2 cup imitation crab, shredded
1 cup cooked and shelled shrimp
   (e.g., 61 to 70 count or Bay shrimp, 150 to 250 count)
6 fresh mushrooms, sliced

In 9 × 13-inch pan or large glass bowl, layer ingredients above in the order listed. Cover and refrigerate overnight.

Before serving, top with:

1-1/2 to 2 cups mayonnaise (spread like frosting)
3 teaspoons sugar (sprinkle over mayonnaise)
1 teaspoon Romano cheese (grated)
Bacon bits for garnish (about 1/4 cup)
2 tomatoes, wedged
2 hard-boiled eggs, chopped

Note: Audrey Yoneshige, my lymphedema therapist, shared this favorite salad with me. She freezes the romano cheese and uses it as needed. Audrey says that, in a pinch, she's prepared the salad that day for a potluck and called it her 6-hour salad. She is often asked for the recipe.

Two-Way Oriental Tuna

yield: 3 servings

* *

1/4 cup mayonnaise
1 tablespoon onion, minced
2 teaspoons curry powder
1 teaspoon lemon juice
1 teaspoon soy sauce
1 can tuna (6 oz.), drained and flaked
1 can water chestnuts (8 oz.), drained and sliced
3 heads Mānoa lettuce, cut into large
    bite-sized pieces, refrigerate
1 to 2 tomatoes, quartered or sliced

Combine first 5 ingredients; blend. Add tuna and water chestnuts; mix together. Chill tuna mixture. Arrange chilled crisp lettuce on individual plates. Place 1/2 cup serving of tuna mixture on lettuce. Arrange tomato quarters or slices as desired.

Note: I got this recipe from Terry Arakaki when we were both teaching at Kainalu Elementary about twenty years ago and I am still using it. I have never seen this recipe anywhere else and I am so happy to include it in this cookbook. Now I know I'll always have it.

Variation: Another way to use Two-Way Oriental Tuna is to spread tuna mixture on 6 to 8 thin slices of French bread. Top with slices of Monterey Jack cheese and broil 2 to 3 inches from heat until cheese is lightly browned. So ono!

Sides

Warabi Appetizer

yield: 8–10 servings

* *

1 bunch warabi (about 30 stalks)
1 cup boiling water
1 package shredded codfish (1.75 oz.)
1/2 onion, thinly sliced
2 firm tomatoes, cubed

Dressing:

1/4 cup soy sauce
1/2 cup sugar
2/3 cup lemon juice (about 4 lemons)
1/4 teaspoon garlic salt

Wash warabi under running water, removing "hair" follicles. Cut into 1-inch lengths. Cook warabi in boiling water for 1 to 2 minutes or until tender; drain and immediately place in ice cold water. Drain and set aside.

Soak codfish in water for 10 to 15 minutes; drain and shred. Combine warabi, codfish, onion and tomatoes in mixing bowl. Mix dressing ingredients together and pour over warabi mixture; toss gently. Chill before serving.

Baked Beans

yield: 8–10 servings

* *

4 slices bacon, chopped
1 onion, chopped
1 small Portuguese sausage (5 oz.), sliced
1 can pork and beans (15 oz.)
1 can kidney beans (15 oz.), drained
1 can pinto beans (15 oz.), drained
1/2 cup brown sugar, or less, as desired
1/3 cup catsup
2 teaspoons Worcestershire sauce
1/4 cup mild cheddar cheese, grated
Parmesan cheese for sprinkling

Fry bacon until lightly browned. Add onion and Portuguese sausage and cook together until onion is tender. In large bowl, mix together all ingredients (except for the cheeses) and place in greased casserole dish. Top with cheddar and parmesan cheese. Bake at 350°F for 1 hour.

Bitter Melon with Tofu

yield: 6 servings

* *

1 bitter melon, cut in half lengthwise,
    seeded and sliced diagonally
2 tablespoons oil
1 leek, diagonally sliced
2 to 3 pieces shiitake, soaked and sliced, discard stem
1 container firm tofu (20 oz.), drained and cut into cubes
1 cup Chinese roast pork, thinly sliced
2 eggs, beaten

Seasoning:

1 tablespoon sake
3 tablespoons soy sauce
1-1/2 teaspoons salt
Pepper to taste

Heat oil and add bitter melon. Stir-fry on high heat until lightly browned and slightly softened. Move bitter melon to side of skillet and add leeks. When leeks are browned, add shiitake mushrooms and stir-fry together. Add tofu, roast pork and seasoning. Cook on high heat. Pour beaten eggs over and allow to coat and cook thoroughly. Be careful not to overcook. Serve immediately.

Bread and Butter Pickles

yield: 6 quarts

* *

8 pounds cucumbers (medium size), cut into thin
    round slices (about 1/4-inch thick)
6 medium round onions, sliced round (or cut in
    half first, then sliced)
1 green pepper, finely chopped
3 cloves garlic, chopped
3 trays ice cubes
3/4 cup Hawaiian salt

Syrup:

5 cups sugar
3 cups vinegar
1-1/2 teaspoons turmeric
1-1/2 teaspoons celery seed
2 teaspoons mustard seed

Combine cucumbers, sliced onions, green pepper and chopped garlic in very large container. Cover with ice cubes and add salt. Let stand for 3 hours. Mix a few times. Drain thoroughly.

Combine syrup ingredients. Boil to boiling point and pour over cucumbers. Place in glass containers and refrigerate.

Note: This is the best bread and butter pickle recipe! My mother made this when I was little and everyone loves it when I make it now. It's crunchy and great for sandwiches. It makes a lot but they'll disappear very quickly.

Choi Sum

yield: 3–4 servings

* *

1 bunch choi sum (about 3/4 pound)
1 tablespoon oil
2 cloves garlic, crushed
Pinch Hawaiian salt
1/2 cup water
1 tablespoon oyster sauce (optional)

Wash choi sum and cut into 3-inch lengths. Heat skillet on medium high, add oil and stir-fry garlic until lightly browned. Add choi sum; stir-fry until wilted and bright green in color. Sprinkle salt and add 1/2 cup water. Cover, lower heat, and simmer about 2 to 3 minutes or until choi sum is cooked tender, stirring occasionally. Mix in oyster sauce, if desired, or pour over choi sum in serving dish for stronger flavor.

Note: I don't remember ever eating choi sum until I married Don and became part of a Chinese family. My mother-in-law, Ellen Hee, showed me how to prepare many family favorites and now choi sum is one of my favorite vegetable dishes! We eat this frequently. I also use this procedure for stir-frying watercress, mustard cabbage, and ong choy.

Colcannon

yield: 8–10 servings

* *

8 medium baking potatoes
1 head curly kale, tough ribs removed and finely chopped
(about 1/2 pound)
1-1/4 cups milk
6 stalks green onions, finely sliced
1 tablespoon parsley, chopped
1/8 teaspoon thyme (or 1/2 teaspoon fresh thyme)
8 tablespoons butter, divided

Peel potatoes, place in saucepan and cover with cold salted water. Bring to boil and cook 20 minutes, or until done. Drain and let potatoes dry. Hand mash; set aside.

In a 2-quart pot, boil salted water and add kale. Cook about 25 minutes or until tender; drain and set aside.

In large pot, over medium-low heat, heat milk with green onions, parsley and thyme, stirring frequently. Add kale to milk. Simmer for 3 minutes. Add mashed potatoes and stir in 4 tablespoons butter. Mix to a smooth creamy consistency. Place into a serving dish. If desired, make a well in the center and place remaining butter in the well and serve.

Note: Roger Pflum from Hilo is of part Irish ancestry and shared this traditional Irish dish, a real comfort food. This is a great potluck dish for St. Patrick's Day as the kale turns the mashed potatoes a green color.

Suggestion: Try 2 lightly fried eggs on top of the colcannon.

Note: Somewhere I read about a simple rule to remember while cooking vegetables. Those grown below the ground should be started in cold salted water while those grown above the ground should be started in boiling salted water. The recipe above is a good example.

Eggplant with Den Miso

yield: 6–8 servings

* *

1 pound Japanese eggplant (about 4 long-type eggplants)
1 tablespoon oil
2 teaspoons Den Miso (recipe follows)

Cut eggplant diagonally into 1/2-inch to 1-inch slices and soak in water. Drain and pat dry with paper towels. Heat oil in skillet and fry eggplant until softened and both sides are browned. Add more oil as needed. Place eggplant on serving platter and spread 2 teaspoons Den Miso evenly over cooked eggplant.

Den Miso:

2 cups white miso
1 cup sake
1 cup Mirin cooking wine
1 cup sugar

Blend miso with sake until smooth. Then add rest of ingredients and cook in double boiler over simmering water. Cook for 50 minutes, stirring almost constantly. Cool and refrigerate up to 12 months (color of miso will naturally darken). Makes about 6 cups.

Note: I got this recipe from Amy Hee who says that Den Miso is also great for marinating seafood. For example, marinate butterfish with Den Miso for 2 days. Place fish on foil and broil in oven. Broil one side until browned. Flip over and place directly on broiler pan. Discard foil. Continue broiling until browned.

Gobo with Watercress

yield: 6–8 servings

✳ ✳

1/2 to 1 pound lean pork, thinly sliced
2 tablespoons oil
2 cloves garlic, chopped
1/2 onion, sliced
1 frozen package of gobo (10 oz.), thawed
1 large carrot, cut into matchstick-sized pieces
4 tablespoons soy sauce
2-1/2 tablespoons sugar
1 bunch watercress, cut into 2-inch lengths
1 teaspoon crushed red pepper, adjust to taste

Heat oil in large frying pan; stir-fry garlic and onion. Add pork and stir-fry until pork is browned. Add frozen gobo and carrots; cook for 10 to 15 minutes. Add soy sauce and sugar; cook until pork is glazed. Add watercress and red pepper. Cook until watercress is softened to your taste.

Note: Using frozen gobo is time-saving and this recipe is very easy and tasty. However, if possible, use fresh gobo for better texture and flavor.

Green Bean Casserole

yield: : 8 servings

* *

2 cans cut green beans (14.5 oz. each), drained
1 can Durkee's® French Fried Onions (2.8 oz.), reserve 1/4 cup
1 can cream of mushroom soup (10-3/4 oz.)
Dash pepper
1 can mushrooms, pieces and stems (6.5 oz.), with liquid
1/2 cup toasted slivered almonds (or less)
2/3 cup cheddar cheese, grated

Mix first 6 ingredients (minus the reserved 1/4 cup french-fried onions) together in bowl. Place in 2-quart casserole dish. Sprinkle the reserved 1/4 cup of french-fried onions over. Then sprinkle the cheddar cheese over all. Bake at 375°F for 30 minutes.

Note: This is traditional for Thanksgiving dinner. My daughter, Cheryl, adapted the original recipe that I gave to her many years ago and her family loves it this way. Cheryl especially likes the crunchy texture of the added amount of toasted slivered almonds.

Zucchini Patties

yield: 8–10 servings

✳ ✳

1 pound zucchini (about 3 zucchini), unpeeled
1 teaspoon salt, for sprinkling
4 tablespoons flour
1 small onion, finely chopped
5 ounces ham or Portuguese sausage, julienned
1/2 teaspoon salt
1/2 teaspoon pepper
4 eggs, beaten
Olive oil or vegetable oil for frying

Use large grater side to grate zucchini. Place in bowl and sprinkle about 1 teaspoon salt over grated zucchini. Toss and let sit 5 minutes. Squeeze out excess water until slightly dry (but not too dry).

Add flour to zucchini and mix. Add onion, meat, salt, pepper and beaten eggs to mixture; mix together.

Heat just enough oil to coat bottom of fry pan. Use a serving spoon and drop zucchini mixture by spoonfuls. Patties should be about 3 inches in size for easy turning. Cook both sides. Add more oil as needed.

Note: Masako Ogata, a spry 85-year-old from Hilo, recommended this recipe especially for senior citizens. She says these patties are tasty and soft to eat. Masako has always enjoyed cooking and she still cooks for her family. She says this recipe is easily reduced for less people.

Green Beans with Miso Sauce

yield: 6 servings

* *

1 pound green beans

Sauce:

1/3 cup mayonnaise
2-1/2 tablespoons miso
1/2 tablespoon sugar, adjust to taste
1-1/2 tablespoons toasted sesame seeds

Cut green beans into 1-1/2-inch pieces and parboil until tender (about 5 to 10 minutes). Drain and cool. Combine sauce ingredients. Mix beans into sauce. Chill for 1 hour.

Note: My neighbor, Ruby Saito, and I love green beans and so she shared this recipe with me. When the green beans are tender, this dish is a favorite!

Hash Brown Potato Casserole

yield: 9 × 13-inch pan

* *

1 package frozen hash brown potatoes, cubed style
    (2 pounds), *do not thaw*
1/4 cup onion, minced
1 can cream of celery soup (10-3/4 oz.)
6 ounces evaporated milk (half of 12-oz. can)
1 package cream cheese (3 oz.), softened
1/2 cup butter, melted (1 block)
1 cup cheddar cheese, grated

Place frozen hash brown potatoes in 9 × 13-inch baking dish. Sprinkle minced onion over potatoes. Mix together cream of celery soup, evaporated milk, cream cheese and melted butter. Pour over potatoes. Sprinkle cheddar cheese over all. Bake at 350°F for 1-1/2 hours.

Note: Really yummy! This goes great with a roast. This recipe was given to me many years ago by my student teacher, Kim Motta, who is a great cook. Thank you, Kim, for all the recipes you shared with me.

Hawaiian Namasu

yield: 12 servings

* *

1/2 pound salted salmon
2 pounds cucumbers
Salt for sprinkling
1 Maui onion, thinly sliced
5 stalks green onions, cut into 3/4-inch lengths
2 tomatoes, diced

Sauce:

1 teaspoon dried shrimp, chopped
3/4 cup sugar
3/4 cup white vinegar
1 tablespoon sake or mirin
1 tablespoon powdered soup stock
   (e.g., 1 envelope S&S® Original Soup Base)

In large bowl, combine sauce ingredients. Mix and let sit until
sugar is dissolved; stir occasionally. Remove skin and bones
from salmon. Cut salmon in small pieces and soak in sauce.

Cut cucumbers in half lengthwise. Remove seeds, slice thinly
and sprinkle liberally with salt. Toss to coat and set aside for
15 minutes. Squeeze excess water from cucumbers and add to
salmon. Add rest of vegetables and mix everything together
and refrigerate to chill before serving.

Hot Garlic Eggplant

yield: 2 servings

* *

**1 large round eggplant, cut into 1-inch-long strips
and placed in water until ready to use**
1/2 cup ground pork
1 cup oil

Sauce:

3 tablespoons soy sauce
2 teaspoons sugar
2 teaspoons vinegar
2 teaspoons fresh ginger, minced
2 cloves garlic, minced
**1/2 Hawaiian chili pepper, crushed
(or 1/4 teaspoon crushed red pepper)**
1 teaspoon cornstarch

Mix together sauce ingredients; set aside.

Heat oil in frying pan until hot. Drain eggplant, pat dry with paper towels and fry in oil until pulp is tender. Place cooked eggplant pieces between paper towels and press lightly to remove excess oil. Add pork to the pan and cook. Remove pork and pour out oil. Heat sauce in pan until near boiling. Add eggplant and pork. Mix together until thoroughly heated. Add a little water if too dry. Serve immediately with hot rice.

Note: This is one of my mother's favorite dishes. She loves eggplant. The recipe is based upon Maple Garden Restaurant's contributing recipe to one of the Chinese Narcissus Beauty Pageant promotions many, many years ago.

Kimpira Gobo with Portuguese Sausage

yield: : 4–5 servings as a side dish

* *

1/2 pound gobo, scraped clean, slivered and soaked in water
1 tablespoon oil
1 tablespoon dried shrimp, minced
1/2 cup Portuguese sausage, cubed
1/4 cup soy sauce
3 tablespoons sugar
1/8 teaspoon crushed red pepper
1/8 teaspoon cayenne pepper
Dash pepper

Heat oil and sauté shrimp. Drain gobo and add to shrimp; stir-fry 1 minute. Add remaining ingredients and continue cooking over medium heat until sauce is absorbed.

Variation: Slivered carrots may be added for color.

Note: Very delicious! I tried several other recipes and found this kimpira most tasty of all. It's easy to prepare using simple ingredients.

Korean Cucumbers

yield: 10–12 servings

* *

2 pounds Japanese cucumbers, unpeeled.

Cut cucumbers into bite-sized pieces and soak in iced cold water for about 1 hour; mix frequently. Drain.

Marinade:

1/2 cup sugar
1/2 cup soy sauce
1/2 cup vinegar
1 teaspoon wine vinegar
1/2 cup green onion, thinly sliced
2 cloves garlic, minced
1/2 teaspoon salt
1 small Hawaiian chili pepper, seeded and chopped
1/2 teaspoon black pepper
1 teaspoon sesame oil

Combine marinade ingredients and mix with cucumbers. Refrigerate overnight.

Korean Potatoes

yield: 6 servings

* *

3 medium potatoes (about 2 pounds)
2 cups water
1 tablespoon Hawaiian salt

Soy Sauce Mixture:

1 cup water
1/4 cup sugar
1/4 cup low-sodium soy sauce
1 tablespoon garlic, minced
1/2 teaspoon pepper (or less, adjust to taste)
1 tablespoon vegetable oil

Peel and cut potatoes into bite-sized pieces. Immerse in brine of water and salt for 10 minutes; drain. Place potatoes in skillet and pour soy sauce mixture over. Cook, uncovered, over medium-high heat 10 to 20 minutes, stirring occasionally, until tender.

Note: Very tasty and similar to the cooked potatoes served at Korean take-outs in various malls.

Kurome

yield: 6–8 servings

* *

1 package kurome (1.5 oz.)
4 medium shiitake, softened and thinly sliced
1 teaspoon oil
1-1/2 tablespoons dried shrimp, chopped
1 block konnyaku (one of two pieces in
    konnyaku container), cut into thin strips
1 aburage (one of four pieces in 2-oz. package),
    cut into thin strips
1/3 cup sugar
1/3 cup soy sauce

Rinse kurome in water 3 times and soak until softened, about 3 hours; drain. Heat oil in nonstick skillet and sauté dried shrimp for 1 minute. Stir in kurome. Add konnyaku, aburage and shiitake and continue stirring until cooked (about 5 minutes). Mix together sugar and soy sauce and add to kurome mixture. Stir until heated through. Cook for 15 more minutes (uncovered) on medium low, stirring occasionally.

Lemongrass Tofu

yield: 4 servings

* *

1 block firm tofu (12 oz.), cubed and drained
2 lemongrass stalks
1 teaspoon oil
1/2 cup round onion, sliced
2 shallots, thinly sliced (optional)
1 clove garlic, minced
1-1/2 tablespoons nuoc mam (fish sauce)
2 teaspoons sugar
1 Hawaiian chili pepper, chopped (adjust to taste)

Remove tough outer layers of lemongrass and upper two-thirds of stalk; crush. Combine sugar, nuoc mam and chili pepper; set aside.

Heat oil in nonstick skillet over medium-high heat. Add onion, shallots and garlic; stir-fry about 1 minute. Lower heat to medium and add lemongrass, tofu and nuoc mam mixture. Cook and stir until onion is crisp-tender. Remove and discard large pieces of lemongrass.

Long Rice and Vegetables

yield: 4 servings

* *

2 packages long rice (1-3/4 oz. each)
1/2 can chicken broth (half of 14-1/2-oz. can)
1 cup water
1 tablespoon oil and 1/2 teaspoon sesame oil
1 clove garlic, chopped
1/2-inch slice fresh ginger
2 shiitake mushrooms, soaked and sliced
1 carrot, slivered
1/4 onion, sliced
2 stalks green onion, cut into 2-inch lengths
1/2 teaspoon salt

Sauce:

1/2 can chicken broth
1 tablespoon mirin
1 tablespoon soy sauce
1 teaspoon oyster sauce
1/2 teaspoon sugar

Boil long rice in 1/2-can chicken broth and 1 cup water for 3 minutes or until softened. Drain and set aside. Cut into 3-inch lengths.

Stir-fry garlic and ginger in oil. Add vegetables and salt. Cook until tender. Mix sauce ingredients and add in vegetables. Remove ginger. Add long rice. Cook for 2 minutes.

Variation: Add cooked shredded chicken or gobo tempura slices to long rice.

Note: Another favorite dish of my mother's. My mother loves long rice cooked in many ways.

Hijiki

yield: 12 servings

* *

1 package hijiki (3 oz.)
1/4 cup oil
2 pieces aburage, finely sliced
1/2 cup soy sauce
1/3 cup sugar
1/4 cup mirin
1/4 cup sesame seeds

Soak hijiki for 2 to 4 hours. Squeeze out water. Heat oil and fry hijiki. Add aburage, soy sauce, sugar and mirin and cook on high heat until liquid is absorbed. Mix in sesame seeds.

Variation: Substitute kurome for hijiki.

Maui Onion

yield: 2 quarts

* *

2-1/2 pounds onions (about 6 onions), cut into quarters
2 to 4 Hawaiian chili peppers, crushed

Sauce:

1/2 cup sugar
1 handful Hawaiian salt
1-1/4 cups cider vinegar

Place onions and 1 to 2 chili peppers in each quart jar. Mix sauce ingredients and pour over onions. Let stand overnight, then refrigerate.

Note: Another easy and great recipe from my neighbor, Evie Shiraki. Evie got this recipe from a good friend and she says it's foolproof!

Namul

yield: 6 servings as a side dish

* *

1 package bean sprouts (10 oz.)
1 bunch watercress, cut into 2-inch lengths
Water for boiling

Bring about 3 cups water to boil; mix in bean sprouts. After 1 minute, drain and rinse with cool water. Drain and squeeze out excess water and place bean sprouts in bowl. Boil another 3 cups water. Put in watercress and cook about 2 to 3 minutes. Drain and rinse with cool water. Drain thoroughly. Place in bowl with bean sprouts.

Sauce:

2 tablespoons sesame seeds
1 teaspoon sugar
3 to 4 tablespoons soy sauce
1 tablespoon sesame oil
1 tablespoon green onion
Dash black pepper

Mix sauce ingredients. Pour over bean sprouts and watercress and lightly toss together.

Note: Dot Inoue, who is of Korean descent, was a great cook and seamstress. She handed down many of her recipes to her daughter, Evelyn, who is now sharing them with us.

Nishime

yield: 6–8 servings

* *

4 pieces chicken thighs, boneless and skinless
1 tablespoon oil
2 cans chicken broth (14-1/2 oz. each)
4 pieces dried mushrooms, soaked and sliced
1 package nishime konbu (1 oz.)
1 container konyaku (10 oz.), cut into 3/4-inch x 1-inch pieces
1 can bamboo shoots (8.5 oz.), cut into 1-inch pieces
1/2 cup soy sauce
2/3 cup sugar (or less)
4 to 5 carrots, cut into 1-inch pieces
1 small daikon (about 1/2 pound), cut into 1-inch pieces
1 cup burdock root (gobo)
2 cups araimo, peeled and cut into 1-1/2-inch pieces
1 can lotus root (7 oz.) or 1/2 pound fresh lotus root
1 package aburage (2 oz.), cut into 1-1/2-inch pieces
1/4 pound Chinese peas, blanched

Wash konbu and tie into knots 1 inch apart. Cut between knots. Scrape burdock root clean and cut into 1/4-inch thick diagonal slices; soak in water until ready to use.

Cut chicken into bite-sized pieces. In large pot, fry chicken in oil until light brown. Add chicken broth, mushrooms, konbu, konyaku and bamboo shoots. Cover and cook for 10 minutes. Add soy sauce and sugar, cover, and cook for 5 minutes. Add carrots, daikon and gobo; cover and cook for 15 minutes. Add araimo, lotus root and aburage. Cover and cook until araimo is fork-tender; toss gently occasionally. Garnish with Chinese peas.

Ogo (Seaweed) Kim Chee

yield: 6–8 servings

* *

1 pound ogo (seaweed)

Sauce:

1/3 cup vinegar
1/4 cup soy sauce
2 tablespoons sugar
1-1/2 teaspoons roasted sesame seeds
1/4 cup green onion, chopped
1 Hawaiian chili pepper, seeded and chopped
1 garlic, grated
1 tablespoon ginger, grated

Clean and parboil ogo. Mix sauce ingredients and pour over ogo. Chill.

Note: This is another recipe from Jean Tanimoto from thirty years ago. It is so ono! It's harder to find the crunchy type of ogo that is best for this dish. But whenever I'm fortunate enough to get hold of some fresh, crunchy ogo, I always make this. It stores well in the refrigerator for several days.

Ong Choy and Harm Ha (Shrimp Sauce)

yield: 4 servings

✳ ✳

1 bunch ong choy (about 1 pound), cut into 2-inch lengths
1 tablespoon oil
1 clove garlic, crushed
Pinch Hawaiian salt
1/2 cup water
1-1/2 teaspoons harm ha (adjust to taste)

Heat oil and sauté garlic. Add ong choy and cook about 3 minutes, stirring occasionally. Add a small pinch Hawaiian salt and water. Cover and simmer about 2 minutes. Add harm ha and continue cooking, uncovered, until ong choy is tender. Stir occasionally.

Note: This is another family favorite which I learned to prepare from my mother-in-law, Ellen Hee, when I first got married. It is a tasty and nutritious vegetable dish. (It does have a distinct aroma so you may wish to begin with less shrimp sauce.)

Oven-Fried Potatoes

yield: 30 potato wedges

* *

5 unpeeled medium-size baking potatoes, cut into 6 wedges

Seasoning:

1/2 cup salad oil
2 tablespoons grated parmesan cheese
1 teaspoon salt
1 teaspoon garlic powder
1/2 teaspoon paprika
1/4 teaspoon pepper

Arrange potatoes, peel side down, in foil-lined shallow baking pan. Mix seasoning ingredients and brush over potatoes. Bake at 375°F for 45 minutes or until potatoes are golden brown and tender. Brush occasionally with oil mixture.

Note: For large potatoes, cut into 8 wedges. For small potatoes, cut into 4 wedges. For faster baking, bake at 400°F about 20 minutes.

Pumpkin

yield: 8–10 servings

* *

2 to 3 pounds pumpkin

Seasoning:

1 to 2 tablespoons dried shrimp, chopped
2 tablespoons sugar
2 tablespoons soy sauce
2 tablespoons sake (or sherry)
1 tablespoon oil
1 cup water
1 to 2 teaspoons fresh ginger, grated
1/2 teaspoon salt

Scrub pumpkin thoroughly. Cut in half and remove seeds. Cut into 2-inch pieces; set aside.

Combine seasoning ingredients in large pot. Cover and bring to boil. Lower heat and simmer, covered, for 5 minutes. Add pumpkin and cook uncovered, tossing pumpkin occasionally, for about 10 minutes or until pumpkin is tender and liquid has evaporated.

Note: Be careful when cutting pumpkin. The kabocha (pumpkin) sold in the supermarket is very dense and heavy. My husband, Don, always helps me. I love pumpkin and I found that sometimes the kabocha can be so sweet and perfect and at other times, watery, or not so sweet. I like the ones that are more orange in color.

Scalloped Potatoes

yield: 12–14 servings

* *

5 to 6 medium potatoes, peeled and thinly sliced
Salt and pepper to taste
1 onion, sliced
1 Portuguese sausage, mild or hot (10 oz.) or ham slices
1 can cream of mushroom soup (10-3/4 oz.)
1 can water (use soup can)

Layer potato slices in greased casserole, sprinkling each layer with salt and pepper and placing onion and meat of choice between layers of potato. Blend soup with water; pour over potato layers. Cover and bake at 350°F for 45 minutes. Uncover and bake for 45 minutes longer or until potatoes are tender and brown.

Sesame Asparagus

yield: 4–5 servings

* *

1 pound asparagus
1 tablespoon salad oil
1 tablespoon vinegar
1 tablespoon soy sauce
4 teaspoons sugar
1 tablespoon roasted sesame seeds
   (or sesame seeds may be ground)

Parboil or steam asparagus. Drain and place on platter. Heat remaining ingredients. Bring to boil and pour over asparagus.

Variation: Broccoli may be substituted for asparagus.

Spicy Chili-Fried Soy Beans

yield: 6 servings

* *

1 pound frozen soy beans, shelled or unshelled
6 to 7 cups water
4 tablespoons peanut oil, divided
1 small Hawaiian chili pepper, seeded and minced
2 tablespoons fresh ginger, minced
3 garlic cloves, minced (about 2 teaspoons)
3 tablespoons low-salt soy sauce
1 tablespoon oyster sauce
1/2 teaspoon sesame oil

Bring water to boil; stir in frozen soybeans. Bring to boil again, stirring soybeans; cook 30 seconds. Test for doneness (beans should be crisp cooked). Drain and set aside.

In large frying pan or wok, heat 2 tablespoons peanut oil until hot and shimmering. Add soy beans and cook, stirring constantly, until beans are heated through (about 2 to 3 minutes).

Push beans aside: add remaining peanut oil and chili pepper and cook 30 seconds. Add ginger and garlic and cook 1 minute. Add soy sauce, oyster sauce, sesame oil and cook, stirring constantly, until liquid is evaporated (about 30 seconds).

Note: A great taste treat! You must try this. The shelled beans are easier to eat with rice and the unshelled ones for pūpū May be served hot or at room temperature.

Special Spinach

* *

2 packages frozen chopped spinach (8 oz. each)
1/4 cup water
1 cup small curd cottage cheese
1-1/2 tablespoons dry onion soup mix (adjust to taste)

Cook spinach in water just until tender. (Do not salt water.) Drain thoroughly, pressing out liquid. Put spinach in saucepan and stir in cottage cheese and onion soup mix. Cook over low heat, stirring occasionally, until mixture is hot.

Spicy Grilled Tofu

yield: 4 servings

* *

1 block firm tofu (20 oz.)
1/4 cup flour
Oil for frying

Sauce:

1/4 cup soy sauce
2 cloves garlic, crushed
2 tablespoons sugar, adjust to taste
2 tablespoons mirin
1/4 cup oil
1 teaspoon ground chili pepper or 2 fresh chili peppers, seeded and minced

Cut tofu in half crosswise. Cut each section into four equal rectangles. Drain well. Dust with flour and pan-fry in oil until golden brown.

Combine sauce ingredients and bring to boil. Serve tofu with sauce.

Stir-Fried Asparagus

yield: 4 servings

* *

1 pound asparagus
2 teaspoons peanut oil
1/2 teaspoon salt (or less)
1/4 teaspoon black pepper (or less)
2 cloves garlic, chopped
1/4 cup chicken broth
1 teaspoon sherry or sake
1-1/2 tablespoons oyster sauce
1 teaspoon sesame oil

Remove "woody" ends of asparagus and cut into thick, diagonal slices. Measure out salt and pepper and, with garlic, set aside. Combine chicken broth, sherry and oyster sauce and set aside.

Heat wok over high heat and swirl in peanut oil until slightly smoking. Toss in salt, pepper and garlic; stir for 30 seconds. Add asparagus and continue to stir-fry for 1 minute. Add broth, sherry and oyster sauce; continue to stir-fry for 3 more minutes or until asparagus is tender to your taste. Drizzle sesame oil along the sides of the wok and stir for 20 seconds more.

Cucumber Namasu

yield: 10–12 servings

✻ ✻

4 Japanese cucumbers, peeled
1 to 2 teaspoons salt (adjust to taste)
1/2 block kamaboko (half of 6 oz.), slivered
1/4 cup fueru wakame

Sauce:

1-1/4 cups sugar
1 cup Japanese vinegar
1 tablespoon salt

Combine sauce ingredients; heat until sugar dissolves. Cool; set aside. (yield: 1-1/2 cups)

Cut peeled cucumbers into 1/2-inch or less round slices. (Use 2 shallow cuts then slice through.) Sprinkle salt over cucumbers, toss and let sit about 30 to 40 minutes. Toss occasionally. (May add more salt if needed.) Drain. Do not squeeze. Let sit, draining, for a short while. (about 15 minutes.) Toss occassionally.

Soak wakame in water for 5 minutes or longer. May be soaked until ready to use. Drain and squeeze out excess water.

Combine cucumber, kamaboko and wakame. Pour about 1 cup sauce over and gently mix together. Reserve remaining sauce. Refrigerate overnight. Add more sauce the next day if needed.

Note: For our New Year's party in Hilo, we always request cucumber namasu from my cousin, Miye Watanabe. Miye shared this popular Hilo Alway of making namasu. Sometimes my mother squeezes in some fresh lemon juice for added flavor.

Variation: Add slivered carrots or thinly sliced parboiled lotus root.

String Beans and Pork

yield: 6–8 servings

* *

1 pound green beans, julienned
1/2 to 1 pound pork, thinly sliced

Sauce:

1/4 cup low-salt soy sauce
2 tablespoons brown sugar
1 clove garlic, diced or crushed
1 teaspoon roasted sesame seeds
1 tablespoon green onion, chopped
Pepper to season

Prepare sauce and marinate pork for 15 to 20 minutes. In frying pan fry pork with sauce ingredients and simmer until pork is cooked. Add green beans and continue cooking, uncovered, until beans are tender. Stir occasionally.

Note: No oil needed when frying pork. Use oil to fry if substituting chicken for pork. This very old favorite green bean recipe was shared by Miss Kim, a teacher at Wheeler Elementary School when we lived in teachers' cottages right on base (circa 1965). Thank you, Leona.

Sweet Potato Tempura

yield: Approximately 5 dozen slices

* *

6 sweet potatoes (about 3 pounds)

Batter:

3 cups flour
1-1/4 cups sugar
1 teaspoon salt
2 tablespoons baking powder
2 eggs
1-1/2 cups water
Oil for deep-frying

Boil potatoes until cooked (about 25 minutes). Use skewer to check for doneness. Do not overcook. Cool and slice into 1/4-inch-thick round slices. Prepare batter. Combine dry ingredients. Add eggs and water; beat until smooth. Dip potato slices in batter and deep-fry. Drain on paper towels.

Takuan

yield: About 2 quarts

* *

4 to 5 pounds long daikon, cut into pieces of your choice
2-1/2 cups sugar
4 tablespoons salt
4 tablespoons Heinz® Vinegar
5 to 10 drops yellow food color (adjust to preference)

Combine sugar, salt and vinegar; place over sliced daikon. Do not mix for 2 hours. Mix after 2 hours and leave for another hour. Add yellow food color; leave for 30 minutes. Place in clean jars and refrigerate.

Suggestion: Daikon may be cut thick or thin, in rounds, half-circles or lengthwise. For a little spicy flavor, add Hawaiian chili peppers to your taste.

Note: Dot Inoue recommended selecting young daikon, the ones that are usually small and slender. Daikon may be peeled or not peeled. Leaving the skin on gives it an extra crunch.

Tofu and Kim Chee Stir-Fry

yield: 4–6 servings

* *

1 block tofu (20 oz.)
2 tablespoons oil
Salt to taste
1 cup won bok kim chee
2 tablespoons mirin
2 teaspoons soy sauce
1 cup chives or green onions, cut into 2-inch lengths
2 eggs, beaten

Break tofu into chunks and place on paper towels on microwaveable dish. Warm in microwave about 30 seconds. Pat dry. Heat oil in nonstick pan; fry tofu until crisp on one side. Sprinkle salt to taste. Turn over tofu and fry other side. Remove from pan; set aside. Add a little more oil and stir-fry kim chee until hot; add tofu. Add mirin and soy sauce; carefully toss. Add chives or green onions and cook until limp. Pour beaten eggs over to bind everything together. Cover and cook for a few minutes until eggs are just cooked.

Tsukemono

yield: 1 gallon

* *

1 head cabbage, cut into 8 wedges or fourths

Seasoning:

1 cup sugar
1/4 cup Hawaiian salt
1/4 cup vinegar
1-1/2 cups water
1 tablespoon wine (optional)

Place cabbage in large container. Boil seasoning ingredients and, while hot, pour seasoning over cabbage. Put weight on top to press down. (I use a large bowl filled with water as the weight.) Let soak for 3 to 4 hours at room temperature. Place cabbage with liquid in gallon jar and refrigerate. May be served next day. Rinse and squeeze out water. Chop into pieces and serve as a side dish. Will keep refrigerated for one week.

Note: Daikon or cucumber may be substituted for cabbage. For other vegetables, cool mixture first. This old recipe is from Mrs. Mikami, our good friend and neighbor from our 'Amauulu camp days.

Vegetable Lasagna

yield: 9 × 13-inch pan

* *

1 clove garlic, chopped
1 tablespoon oil
1 small onion, chopped
1 green pepper, sliced (optional)
1 can tomato sauce (8 oz.)
1 can stewed tomatoes (14.5 oz.), cut into smaller pieces
1 can "basil, garlic & oregano" tomato paste (6 oz.)
1-1/2 cans water (measure with tomato paste can)
1 envelope spaghetti sauce mix (1.5 oz.)
1 large zucchini, sliced
8 to 10 fresh mushrooms, sliced
2 boxes frozen spinach, thawed and squeezed
    to remove excess water
2 teaspoons salt
1 tablespoon parsley flakes
2 packages shredded mozzarella cheese (8 oz. each)
1 box extra-wide lasagna noodles (8 oz.)

Heat oil; brown garlic slightly. Add onion and cook until tender. Add rest of ingredients (except noodles and cheese) and simmer about 1/2 hour.

Cook noodles according to package directions. Rinse with cold water; drain.

Alternate layers of noodles and vegetable mixture in 9 × 13-inch pan. Begin with layer of vegetable mixture. Place 3 noodles, then 8 ounces mozzarella cheese, 3 noodles, vegetable mixture, 3 noodles, vegetable mixture. Top with mozzarella cheese. Bake at 325°F, uncovered, approximately 30 to 45 minutes or until cheese is lightly browned.

Glossary

* *

aburage	deep-fried tofu, fried bean curd
'ahi	yellowfin tuna, shibi (Japanese)
araimo	Japanese taro, dasheen
bonito	tuna
char siu	roasted sweet red pork
choi sum	Chinese broccoli
Chinese parsley	cilantro
chung choi	preserved salted turnip
daikon	white radish or turnip
dashi	soup stock
edamame	soybeans
fueru wakame	dehydrated seaweed
fu jook	dried bean curd
gobo	burdock root
harm ha	shrimp sauce
Hawaiian salt	coarse sea salt
hijiki	dried black seaweed
hoisin sauce	Chinese miso base sauce
hondashi	powdered soup stock base
iriko	small dried fish
jook	rice soup
kamaboko	steamed fish cake
kim chee	Korean spicy pickled vegetables
kinpira	gobo stir-fry with shoyu and sugar
konbu	dried kelp, kobu
konnyaku	tuber root flour cake
kurome	dried black seaweed
long rice	translucent mung bean noodles
mirin	sweet rice wine
miso	fermented soybean paste
mizuna	mustard spinach

mochi	steamed or pounded rice cake
namasu	vinegar-flavored food
ocean salad	deep sea seasoned seaweed
ogo	Japanese term for seaweed
ong choy	swamp cabbage
oyster sauce	oyster-flavored sauce
panko	Japanese bread crumbs
poke	cut-up pieces of raw fish with seasonings
ponzu	a tart, citrus-based sauce
sake	Japanese rice wine
sambal oelek	ground fresh chili paste
shiitake	dried mushrooms
shoyu	soy sauce
siu mai	Chinese meat and vegetable dumpling
soba	buckwheat noodles
somen	fine wheat flour noodles
suribachi	corrugated bowl for grinding
taegu	spiced flavored codfish
takuan	pickled turnip
tempura	seafood or vegetable, battered and deep-fried
tofu	fresh soybean curd
tsukemono	pickled vegetables
udon noodles	Japanese wheat noodles
wakame	long, curling strands of seaweed
warabi	fern shoot
won bok	Chinese cabbage
won ton pi	thin squares of dough made of flour and eggs

Index

tofu
  Bitter Melon with Tofu, 104
  Lemongrass Tofu, 120
  Miso Soup, 24
  Spicy Grilled Tofu, 131
  Tofu and Kim Chee Stir-Fry, 137
  Tofu Salad, 96
  Warabi Tofu Salad, 85
tomatoes
  24-Hour Lettuce Salad, 98
  24-Hour Salad with Shrimp, 99
  Black Bean Soup, 4
  BLT Salad, 53
  Broccoli Shrimp Salad, 56
  Chicken–Tomato Soup, 7
  Ga Hap Ca, 14
  Hawaiian Namasu, 114
  Lentil and Brown Rice Soup, 22
  Minestrone Soup, 23
  Ono Hamburger Soup, 29
  Pasta Salad, 51
  Soba Salad, 81
  Spaghetti Salad, 86
  Spinach–Tomato–Bacon Salad, 89
  Taco Salad, 93
  Tofu Salad, 96
  Two-Way Oriental Tuna, 100
  Vegetable Lasagna, 139
  Vegetable Soup, 41
  Warabi Appetizer, 102
Tropics Dressing, 66
Tsukemono, 138
Tuna Macaroni Salad, 97

turkey 18
  Chicken or Turkey Salad, 57
  Turkey Chowder, 40
  Two–Way Oriental Tuna, 100

V

Vegetable Lasagna, 139
Vegetable Soup, 41
Vegetable Soup with Spinach, 42
Vegetarian Corn Chowder, 44
Vegetarian Portuguese Bean
  Soup, 45

W

Warabi Appetizer, 102
Warabi Tofu Salad, 85
watercress
  Gobo with Watercress, 109
  Namul, 123
  Seaweed–Soba Salad, 84
  Tofu Salad, 96
  Vegetarian Portuguese Bean
    Soup, 45
  Watercress Egg-Drop Soup, 43
Won Ton Soup, 46

Z

zucchini
  Vegetable Lasagna, 139
  Vegetable Soup, 41
  Zucchini Patties, 111